THE SECRET SERIAL KILLER

THE TRUE STORY OF KIERAN KELLY

Acknowledgements

I would like to sincerely thank RTÉ Radio 1's *Documentary on One* series for allowing me to use the recordings made for the 2016 multi-award-winning production *Anatomy of an Irish Serial Killer* from which this book draws extensively.

Thanks to the spectacular editing talent of Belfast's finest, Gerard Donaghy, who knocked this book into shape when it had none. And thank you to Kate Bohdanowicz for catching the mistakes that were missed.

To Mona, thank you for your patience and support and to my baby Maya, for being my calm night-time companion through long rewrites.

Until the next time!

THE SECRET
SERIAL
KILLER

THE TRUE STORY OF KIERAN KELLY

ROBERT MULHERN

PEN & SWORD
TRUE CRIME

First published in Great Britain in 2019 by
PEN AND SWORD TRUE CRIME
an imprint of
Pen & Sword Books Ltd
Yorkshire - Philadelphia

ISBN 978 1 52672 276 8

Typeset in Sabon 12/15 By
Aura Technology and Software Services, India
Printed and bound in the UK by TJ International.

Pen & Sword Books Ltd incorporates the Imprints of Pen & Sword Books
Archaeology, Atlas, Aviation, Battleground, Discovery, Family History,
History, Maritime, Military, Naval, Politics, Railways, Select, Transport,
True Crime, Fiction, Frontline Books, Leo Cooper, Praetorian Press,
Seaforth Publishing, Wharncliffe and White Owl.

For a complete list of Pen & Sword titles please contact

PEN & SWORD BOOKS LIMITED
47 Church Street, Barnsley, South Yorkshire, S70 2AS, England
E-mail: enquiries@pen-and-sword.co.uk
Website: www.pen-and-sword.co.uk

or

PEN AND SWORD BOOKS
1950 Lawrence Rd, Havertown, PA 19083, USA
E-mail: Uspen-and-sword@casematepublishers.com

Contents

Preface		7
Prologue		8
Chapter 1	Origins	10
Chapter 2	No Good Leads	13
Chapter 3	Officer A	17
Chapter 4	By the Book	19
Chapter 5	Stoke	21
Chapter 6	Mr 999	23
Chapter 7	Captive Audience	28
Chapter 8	Coronation Killer	32
Chapter 9	A Glimpse of Fisher	36
Chapter 10	A Matter of Accuracy	42
Chapter 11	Waldegrave Road	49
Chapter 12	Scratching the Surface	51
Chapter 13	Tube Interchange	54
Chapter 14	School Ties	57
Chapter 15	The Dig	60
Chapter 16	First Confirmation	68
Chapter 17	Through the Roof	71
Chapter 18	Muddied Waters	79

Chapter 19   Remains? What Remains?   85

Chapter 20   Dancing Man   88

Chapter 21   The Tombstone   92

Chapter 22   Fisher   97

Chapter 23   Killing Spree   101

Chapter 24   The Prince and the Pauper   106

Chapter 25   Taking Stock   112

Chapter 26   Lost Archive   115

Chapter 27   Date with the Old Bailey   118

Chapter 28   Appeal   126

Chapter 29   The Verdict   133

Chapter 30   Where are All the Bodies?   136

Chapter 31   Justice Takes Investment   139

Chapter 32   A Seed of Doubt   143

Chapter 33   False Ceiling   146

Chapter 34   Murder in Someone Else's Name   152

Chapter 35   No Right of Reply   156

Chapter 36   Steadying the Ship   159

Chapter 37   Light at the End of the Tunnel?   166

Chapter 38   End of the Line   177

Epilogue   185

Timeline   Kieran Kelly's Significant Dates   190

Due to the nature of the story at hand, this publication cannot be taken to provide the verifiable truth in relation to the Kieran Kelly case. This account endeavours to present the truest version of events as they played out, based on the files and the witnesses that the author had access to whilst researching and writing this book.

Preface

In August 1983, Kieran Patrick Kelly from County Laois in the Irish midlands was arrested for the murder of a homeless man, William Boyd, in the cells of Clapham Police Station, London.

During the interview that followed, Kelly confessed to multiple murders dating back to 1953. But he was only tried and convicted for the manslaughter of Boyd and the murder of another man, Hector Fisher.

Then, in 2015, the Kieran Kelly story was resurrected by a former police officer who claimed the Home Office covered up his crimes and he may have murdered up to thirty-one people.

This story is the search for those missing murders.

Prologue

July 2017, and huge, mature trees sway in the breeze of the County Laois countryside. On a quiet lane that sets off winding into even deeper greenery, two men stand at the start of a driveway to a detached house. It's mid-morning, the sky is brilliant blue in colour and chaff from corn, being harvested in neighbouring fields around the small village of Rathdowney, speckles the air.

The house belongs to a man called Nicky Meagher and this July morning, Nicky's eyes are fixed to the ground close to the entrance. There's a second man beside him whose eyes are also fixed to the ground. Niall O'Doherty is a retired doctor who practised for decades in Rathdowney, just a couple of hundred yards back down the road from where both men are standing.

'That's the spot there now,' said Nicky Meagher, straightening his back. 'That's the spot where the skeleton was found,' he pointed. The drone of a distant lawnmower filled the void left behind by his declaration.

Meagher explained how it was a similar kind of a day back in 1993 when he found the skeleton. He'd been digging a trench for a water pipe to run the fifty or so paces from his home to the road. His son, whom he refers to as Young Nick, was helping him the same afternoon when they struck something hard beneath the surface.

'It was a bone,' he said, his eyes remaining fixed on the ground. 'And then there was a skull, with a wire noose around the neck. I called Niall here.' Meagher looked up and nodded his head in the direction of the doctor. 'And then I called the Gardaí. I'm not sure who arrived first, Niall or the police but I explained to the Gardaí that a convicted murderer, Kieran Kelly, once lived *here*, in this house.

'I knew he lived in London then and the Gardaí joked that the discovery might mean they'd have to travel to London, and that it might mean they'd get to take in a football match.'

Then Nicky Meagher made a long exhale and looked up. 'The Gardaí just packed up and took the remains away, and that was the last we ever heard of it.'

Chapter 1

Origins

It was late evening in July 2015 at London Bridge Station, central London. The setting sun had turned the sky orange over the west of the city and as the daytime temperature dropped, a symphony of screeching train wheels rose up from the platforms that stretched out like long promenades from the station concourse. Rushing beside a stream of city commuters, I hurried into the rear of a train carriage, slumped into a seat and fixed a pair of headphones to my iPhone.

That afternoon, a former Metropolitan Police officer had appeared on a flagship Irish radio programme called *The Ray D'Arcy Show* to describe a story of murder on the London Underground. I was working as a journalist in London, for the radio documentary unit of Ireland's national broadcaster — RTÉ's *Documentary on One* series, and my producer had emailed the link, asking me to look into it.

'Was the underground once stalked by a serial killer who pushed people from tube platforms to their deaths?' asked the eponymous host.

'Well, a new book reveals how a serial killer from Ireland pushed twelve people on to the tube line in London,' he followed. 'And the author is Geoff Platt, who is in a studio in Manchester. Good afternoon, Geoff.'

'Good afternoon, Ray.'

'Now, who was Kieran Kelly?' asked D'Arcy.

'Kieran Patrick Kelly – he was from County Laois,' started Geoff Platt. 'He was born in 1923 and he came to London in 1953.'

'And when did you first come across him?' asked the broadcaster.

'In Clapham Common, after he was picked up for being drunk on the common,' he replied.

'And it was in the interview room that he confessed to all these murders?' followed D'Arcy.

'That's right.'

'And he confessed to what?' prompted the broadcaster.

'He committed sixteen murders on the tube and four by other methods,' said Platt.

The ex-copper went on to explain that the Irishman, Kieran Kelly, confessed to pushing people from station platforms to their deaths on the London Underground between 1953 and 1983.

And he made a sensational declaration. He said that the reason people were only hearing about these murders now was because the British Government had covered them up. That the crimes were so disturbing the authorities decided that they should be kept from the public. Because if London commuters knew about a killer targeting passengers randomly on the underground, it would have resulted in mass panic. It was a claim and a story that was seized upon by the mainstream media.

'Was the underground once stalked by a serial killer who pushed people from tube platforms to their deaths and then got away with it?' opened a BBC News report that appeared at the top of a Google search. 'This former detective says yes,' it continued.

The video item featured the former policeman, Geoff Platt, dressed in a long coat and travelling in a tube carriage. 'We've seen court papers that say – when being interviewed about another murder – Kelly told police: "I'm your man for this one, but now I've started I want to tell you about some more I've done in the past."'

The report went on to say that the murders had taken place on the Northern Line and named stations such as Stockwell and Clapham North as crime scenes. The same sensational allegation – that the Home Office had told police not to make the information public – was included again. And having been a secret for so long, the story was now a matter of public discourse.

More Google searches revealed that the *Daily Express*, the *Daily Star Sunday*, *The Irish Post*, the *Daily Mail*, *Times*, *Irish Examiner*, *The Huffington Post*, *London Evening Standard* and more had reported the story. But strangely, each publication gave a different murder total, ranging from twelve to twenty-four.

The Met's then chief of police, Sir Bernard Hogan-Howe, had been forced to comment on the reports. During an interview on *BBC London Live* he admitted that he was also mystified as to why no apparent action had been taken at the time. He committed to getting to the bottom of the claims made by the former policeman.

Reading this story on the train from London Bridge, as the carriages snaked south into the deepening orange of the evening sky through New Cross Gate, Brockley and Honor Oak Park, I wondered about the claims and if they were true. Did Britain have a prolific serial killer, one the public knew nothing about?

Chapter 2

No Good Leads

In the weeks that followed Sir Bernard Hogan-Howe's commitment on the BBC, the *Daily Mail* reported that an investigation had been launched into former detective Platt's shocking claims of murder and cover-up. By then, the story of an emigrant killer had penetrated the consciousness of Irish London but at the same time, no one knew of any Kieran Kelly that matched the killer's profile.

I'd spent eight years working as a reporter with the London-based *Irish Post* newspaper. In all that time, I couldn't remember hearing any such story of murder involving an Irish citizen. Nor could anyone else. Yet a visit to the newspaper archives in the British Library revealed reports detailing the fatal stabbing of a man called Hector Fisher and the strangulation of a man called William Boyd. But they were committed by someone named as Kiernan Kelly, not Kieran Kelly, who had been tried and convicted at the Old Bailey in 1984.

After hearing the former detective's radio interview, I started making enquiries. But despite the appearance of a K. Kelly on the public record for murder, there was no shared memory of the case. After blitzing a contacts book that could reduce a big city to a small network and still getting nothing, I was given the contact of someone who was certain to know – Father Frank Ryan.

Father Ryan was from the same county, Laois, that had been reported as Kelly's birthplace. He'd dedicated his life to helping Irish emigrants in Britain through the Irish Council for Prisoners Overseas project and had forged hundreds, maybe thousands, of relationships with locked-up emigrants. Pentonville Prison on the Caledonian Road, Wandsworth Prison, south-west of the River Thames and Wormwood Scrubs in Shepherd's Bush were pillars on his beat; while damp hostels, prison visiting rooms and the basements of derelict buildings used by homeless Irish from King's Cross to Kingston were the furniture of his life in London.

A year after the so-named *Kiernan* Kelly was handed down a life sentence in the Old Bailey, Father Frank Ryan and his colleagues began offering support to Irish prisoners in the British system. The fact that this K. Kelly would have been a high-profile prisoner during the period of Father Ryan's outreach work led me to assume that the two men would have met. So I made an appointment to meet the priest in Costa Coffee on Borough High Street, where on this summer's afternoon, brilliant sunshine streamed through the shop's floor-to-ceiling glass windows.

When Father Ryan arrived through the door he was carrying a small rucksack and sported a high hairline, beaten into retreat by a life in London that started when he arrived in 1974. He came to London the same week as the Guildford pub bombings, 30 miles south-west of the capital. That attack, committed by the IRA, killed five people, injured sixty-five more and shone an uncomfortable security spotlight on an Irish community Kieran Kelly would then have been a part of.

Like thousands of others, Father Ryan felt the close stitching of community life in Ireland loosen when he arrived in London. The city was enormous enough to render redundant the religious and social conformity that sometimes stifled independent expression in Ireland. But Britain's tense atmosphere weighed heavily on the shoulders of these new arrivals.

The priest pulled up a window seat and explained how, during his first week in 1974, he had made his way to a support shelter in Kilburn called Conway House. Today, that old airy building rests quietly behind The Sacred Heart Church, off Quex Road. But not so long ago, Conway House was a finishing school for lives worn weary by hard knocks, tough breaks and the comfort of too much alcohol.

Just a couple of hundred yards away, the High Road in Kilburn teemed with Irish emigrants hustling jobs on construction crews, whose vans screamed down motorways with no canopies and the men had only the caps on their heads for cover. Kilburn spun a low parade of Irish cafes and pubs and the postcode was overrun with Irish workers who lived from pay cheque to pay cheque. This was the London of Father Ryan and Kieran Kelly, the London of the low-skilled emigrant labourer, the London of hard work, late nights, casual violence, fleeting sexual encounters and suspicion.

'The security services used to set up a camera in the upstairs bedroom of a terraced home across the road from Conway House,' said Father Ryan. 'And from the window they'd photograph everyone who came and went. My very first night in London, I slept in a room in Conway House beside Gerry Conlon and Paul Hill from Belfast, both wrongly convicted and later released for the Guildford bombings.'

Back then, Conlon and Hill were just two more people trying to make good on a new life that was finding a bad effort in alcohol and limited opportunity. And as the years passed, Father Ryan helped build a database of people using the hostel but often, emigrants – embarrassed by their circumstances – checked in under made-up names and hid behind nicknames. 'Some people were on the run. Others didn't want to be known. More didn't want to be found,' he said.

But an Irishman convicted of two killings, who was tried in Britain's most famous court, is someone Father Frank Ryan *must* have come across? However, his reaction was unexpected and terrifying for the fact that a convicted murderer could hide behind the veil of anonymity and target a community ignored by society. 'I can't remember that I did,' he said. 'I worked with people from the same background, who had the same problems. But I've no recollection of meeting any such person, or even hearing about it. If I did, I'm certain I would remember.'

I explained how one of the contacts I'd reached out to prior to this meeting was his one-time colleague, Father Bobby Gilmore, who'd helped establish the Irish Council for Prisoners Overseas project. Only *he* wasn't familiar with the name linked to the case either. No one, it seemed, could remember the killer that former police officer Geoff Platt had been telling the world about. Not Father Frank Ryan. Not Father Bobby Gilmore. Not landmark hostels such as St Mungo's, based south of the river and with a database dating back to the 1980s. Not journalists and long-time photographers who once worked with Britain's Irish newspapers of record.

And in 2015, the trigger of international news coverage in the UK, Ireland and the US spiked no recall among the emigrant community from which the killer hailed. This, despite a commitment from London's chief of police to get to the bottom of the allegations that an unknown Irishman was at the centre of an alleged cover-up by the Home Office. This, despite a promise from the same police force to revisit the case files.

That summer's afternoon, Father Ryan put a full stop to the long line of phone calls made to Irish contacts. 'I'm sorry I can't help you,' he said. 'I really wish I could.' It was beginning to feel as though Kieran Kelly, the London Underground serial killer, had been magicked into the mainstream out of nowhere. And the only person who seemed to know anything was the ex-detective Geoff Platt, who I was so far unable to contact.

Chapter 3

Officer A

The telephone rang and rang before the receiver lifted with the sound of a click that was followed by a long, weary sigh. 'Helloooo,' exhaled a man's voice at the other end of the line. It was shortly after 9am on a weekday morning in June 2016, and the voice sounded worn, either from years of service, or the start of another week.

The voice belonged to a security source that I'd been told might be in a position to check information on the Kieran Kelly case. 'All these cases were investigated in the 1980s,' he sighed again, after I asked. 'But,' I persisted, 'there is evidence that someone named Kieran Kelly committed a murder, or more than one murder?'

'Oh yeah,' he replied. 'He was charged with more than one.'

It was now almost a year since The Met's chief of police, Sir Bernard Hogan-Howe, declared on the BBC that he would 'get to the bottom of' Geoff Platt's claims of a government cover-up and a serial killer on the London Underground. 'It's my understanding that the process is ongoing,' said the security source. Police officers were continuing to revisit old case files flagged up by Platt in an effort to verify resolved and unresolved crimes from the period highlighted, which was 1953 to 1983.

'These offences, well, a detective inspector who worked on the case came in to speak to us and he gave a full recollection of those,' said the source, who declared his wish to remain anonymous and is identified as Officer A.

'There was a proper investigation at the time and Kieran Kelly was charged for two killings. William Boyd, who he strangled in the cells of Clapham Police Station on 4 August 1983, he was found guilty at the Central Criminal Court for that. And Hector Fisher, who was stabbed and beaten to death on Clapham Common in 1975. And for this Kelly was sent to prison.

'It's been handed over to the Met now and I can tell you some of the facts, but they wouldn't want me commenting on their investigations back in the 1980s.'

'Would the original investigators talk,' I asked?

'They may well do,' Officer A replied. 'I'm not sure what you'd get, and it's not for me to second guess Mr Platt.'

'I've been trying to contact him – Platt,' I said. 'But I haven't been able to so far. Does he live in London?'

'No, in the Midlands,' he said. 'Platt came to see us and he explained his history in the force. We looked into it and, well, some parts of his story don't quite add up.'

'But there is some truth to it,' I followed, thinking again of the reported murder count that varied between twelve and twenty-four.

'Oh yeah,' he replied. 'But the big problem with this case is trying to sort the fact from the fiction.'

Chapter 4

By the Book

'HELLOOOO,' boomed the voice at the end of the phone. 'I believe you're the gent I've just sent a text to?' It was less than a couple of hours since I'd asked Officer A to make contact with Geoff Platt, the ex-copper who had brought this story of cover-up and murder into the public arena, and Platt had texted his telephone number to my mobile.

'So, how can I help you then?' he asked boisterously, after I called. I explained that I'd been trying to make contact to talk to him about Kieran Kelly. 'Well, what you need is my new book,' he declared.

'You mean *The London Underground Serial Killer*?' I asked.

'No, no. That was about my relationship with Kieran Patrick Kelly over two years when he was kept in solitary and I was the only person he had to talk to. I spoke to him two minutes after his final murder and this week, I finished another book about where he was born and how we met. I met his family and kids when he never did. This book is called *The Life of Kieran Kelly*. It's due to be published in August.'

I told Platt I'd called every contact in London and that he seemed to be the only one with ownership of the story. 'Well, I *was* the last person to talk to him,' he replied. 'But yessss,' he sighed. 'There. You. Go.'

I asked if we could meet. His revelations about a prolific secret serial killer had caught the attention of London's emigrant Irish community. It was important to get the story right.

'I'm ducking and diving between London, Edinburgh and I've a place in the Midlands also,' he replied. 'I've been a detective all my life. I've actually a contract for a film on Kelly,' he mused. I offered to travel to meet him.

'OK,' he replied. 'There's a hotel directly opposite the train station at Stoke-on-Trent. They do a three-course lunch for a fiver. Do you reckon your expenses can cover that?' he laughed. 'You can fall off the train, come for lunch, fall back on the train again and be back down to London. It's less than ninety minutes if you book the Virgin train.'

Before signing off, Platt explained that he was going through a lengthy and costly divorce and he gave me another number to contact him on. Then I asked him if he knew of anyone else with close links to the Kelly case. 'I'm the only person alive who really knows him,' he replied.

Chapter 5

Stoke

Less than a handful of commuters were waiting on the concourse of Stoke-on-Trent train station when the 10.15am from London made its slow stuttering entrance. It was an unseasonably cool June morning and a breeze blew under the platform canopy, sending an empty can of coke rattling off down the platform in the direction of London.

Stepping from the door of the train on to the platform, I spotted the North Stafford Hotel in the foreground, where I'd arranged to meet Geoff Platt. It was an old redbrick building, topped with a tall chimney, less than 200 yards from the station. A short, paved walkway lined with benches led up to the hotel entrance and a well-built man was sitting slightly hunched on one of the benches close to the entrance. He was staring off into the distance.

As I got nearer, I recognized the man from news reports as Geoff Platt, but the former beat copper wasn't dressed in the long coat and tie that featured in the televised BBC package. Instead, he wore a blue fleece and baggy, loose-fitting jeans. There was a small sports bag by his feet.

He eased what looked like a 6ft 4in frame off the bench. He offered his hand to shake but appeared hesitant and significantly less certain than the confident voice that had boomed down the telephone line just days earlier. I suggested we talk in the hotel. 'Sure, yes, no problem,' he said, making a deliberate turn in the direction of the hotel entrance.

Inside, the reception was lined with thick carpet and leaked what sounded like the classic 1980s signature tunes of Smooth FM. Platt asked the receptionist if there was somewhere quiet to talk. She smiled and pointed in the direction of a bright, adjoining room that opened into a rectangle of white walls and tall windows that framed the now breaking sunshine.

'This is quiet,' said Platt, settling himself into a brown bucket-shaped leather chair. 'My grandmother owned a good chunk of Stoke,' he added in an almost whisper. 'Yessss,' he exhaled, 'she sold up for £400,000 in 1937. That would make £4 million today. She used to bring us up here and we seemed to be related to everyone. And then I moved up here and started writing books.

'A lot of people talk about serial killers and talk about their books, but I met Kelly ten minutes before his last murder and got to know him. I had the chance to speak to him, to get under his skin and I decided to write a full biography. I found the names of his children, his National Insurance number, his army service number. I found my original notes.' I presumed it was these notes that he'd brought in the sports bag.

'He was in the army?' I asked. 'Oh, not for long,' Platt mused. 'He joined at 22. He had a choice between the Defence Forces in Ireland and the British Army, and he joined the British Army because they had better kit.' Then he paused for a moment, clasped his hands and looked out the window.

Chapter 6

Mr 999

'RANGER 500? RANGER 500! You are not to attend the scene, over.'

To the best of Geoff Platt's memory, it was a Sunday morning in the mid-1980s and he was on patrol in a Metropolitan Police vehicle codenamed Ranger 500, which was equipped and designed to deal with emergency incidents related to gun crime in the city. Platt was behind the steering wheel and driving in the direction of Barnet, north London when sketchy details of a violent attack in Kentish Town on a fellow police officer crackled over the open police communication channel.

'This is Ranger 500,' replied Platt upon hearing the appeals of the police inspector in the control room. 'Am I to understand that this officer is being attacked by a man with an axe?'

'Yes, Ranger 500,' replied the controller.

'Are there other officers with suitable equipment on the way?'

'No Ranger 500!'

'In which case, Ranger 500 *will* be attending, OVER.'

'Ranger 500, you are not to attend the scene, OVER! Ranger 500, this is the inspector in the control room and this call is being recorded. Will you please give your name, divisional number and your warrant number? You are being disciplined and you will face a court martial.'

Sitting in the reception room in the North Stafford Hotel, Platt said he did consider what repercussions he might face for defying this direction from his superior. Non-compliance would constitute a serious breach, but a fellow officer armed with nothing but a standard issue 14-inch police truncheon was being threatened by an axeman.

So Platt pulled hard on the steering wheel and threw Ranger 500 into a U-turn. Then he pressed down with his foot on the accelerator and sped off in the direction of Kentish Town. The police communication channel exploded with commands to turn back. Platt ignored them and arrived into Kentish Town just in time to find his lightly armed colleague in retreat from the axeman.

He swung Ranger 500 into the middle of the altercation and when the vehicle screeched to a halt, he pulled up the handbrake, released the handle on the door and launched his burly frame clear of the driver's seat and out into the street. Behind him Ranger 500's walkie-talkie swung back and forth, as if powered by the urgent appeals of officers in the control room.

'STAND DOWN, RANGER 500! STAND DOWN!'

On the street in Kentish town, Platt pulled out his gun as the axeman turned to engage him. Back at base, officers strained their ears to try and hear what was happening at the far end of a communication channel. Slow seconds turned into long minutes – and then the handset crackled. 'So, what do you want me to do with this axe, then?' boomed Platt's voice through the receiver.

* * *

Platt leaned back into his leather chair in the North Stafford Hotel. Diana Ross was singing on the hotel's sound system.

Upside down.
Boy, you turn me.
Inside out.
And round and round.

The former policeman took a sip of water as I tried to make sense of this whimsical opening salvo, which felt like a bizarre starting point to the Kelly story from a former investigating officer, but it was obviously leading somewhere.

'It was Christmas day in 1984,' he said, leaning forward again. 'FOXTROT 2! FOXTROT 2!' said Platt, adjusting his voice to mimic the order that had come over the police communication channel. 'Can you immediately dispatch to the Good Companion Public House?'

'So there was a guy called John Twomey,' he said, breaking from the impersonation. 'He was a first division armed robber and he had found out who grassed him up for his most recent armed robbery.

'He'd been sent to prison for that, and they are big hard animals these armed robbers – especially someone like him, who has been a lifetime armed robber. He went down to the pub to beat the guy up and would you believe he took his wife with him? I mean, if you are going to square someone up, would you take your wife along? I can't foresee any circumstances where you would take the wife along.'

I know you got charm and appeal, continued Diana Ross in the background.

You always play the field.
I'm crazy to think you are all mine.
As long as the sun continues to shine.
There's a place in my heart for you.
That's the bottom line.

'So, Twomey accused this guy of grassing him up and his wife tossed ammonia in his face,' he said. 'The guy goes down and she brings out an 18-inch hunting knife and buries it between his shoulders, and then Twomey brings out a shotgun and cuts the man in half. I turned up and nicked him and you can imagine, he's still waving the bloodstained knife and shotgun – well, *she* is – when I get there.'

Platt then jumped from that story to an explanation that he was one of a handful of officers assigned to the Met's armed response unit in the 1980s. Dealing with violent criminals was part of his brief. He recalled gun battles, violent arrests, and the names and faces of many he arrested through a career that he said earned him a commendation for his work on the Kieran Kelly case.

With the recorder running and the conversation less than twenty minutes old, I had to remind myself that it had been confirmed by Officer A that these bizarre stories aside, Platt was a part of the original investigation into killings committed by Kelly. There was obviously some substance in the ex-copper's claims that Kelly killed more people than the two he was convicted of. Otherwise, why would the police be conducting an investigation?

'When did you first meet Kieran Kelly?' I asked.

'In 1983,' he replied, quick as a flash.

'I was 28 and a beat copper. I was assigned to the Brixton robbery squad. I was living in Croydon with my new wife and was hoping to get my exams and become a detective.'

That summer in 1983, when Platt was preparing for his exams, he recalled that Kieran Kelly and another man, Paul McManus, had been hanging around the high road in Clapham, looking to score change to buy a cheap bottle of wine or some high-strength lager. This was something of an occupational hazard for a street drinker. In 1983, begging and rough sleeping were illegal in the UK.

Margaret Thatcher's Conservative government had cracked down hard on crime and the vagrancy laws gave Platt and his colleagues the power to arrest homeless people on the street. This drove rough sleepers and street drinkers into the damp basements and derelict buildings frequented by Father Frank Ryan, or to the cover of London's green spaces. And on an uneventful afternoon in August, a call came through to Clapham Police Station that a man had been robbed of a ring on the nearby common.

The man had been relaxing on a bench when Kieran Kelly had sat down beside him. Some kind of physical altercation had taken place and Kelly twisted the man's arm around his back before skillfully whipping a ring from the man's little finger. When the police arrived, they arrested both Kelly and McManus and hauled them down to Clapham Police Station for questioning.

Earlier that day, police officers had nicked a homeless man called William Boyd, possibly for being in breach of those same strict vagrancy laws. He'd been placed in a cell to dry out and it was decided that instead of using a sterile cell that would later have to be cleaned, it would be easier to put Kelly and McManus into the same cell as Boyd. And that's what they did, but by around 5pm screams could be heard throughout the station. According to Platt, officers raced to the cells where they found Boyd on his back.

'The guy was making too much noise,' declared the former detective from his chair in the North Stafford Hotel. 'Kelly told the guy to shut up and he wouldn't, so he took his socks off and wrapped them around Boyd's neck and killed him. And McManus started shouting to be let out.

'Kelly was taken from the cells and immediately confessed to the murder. But he also went on to describe other murders he committed. It took people by surprise. I mean, I remember thinking that if he was telling the truth then it was going to take an awful lot of work by officers to prove it.

'It was my job to bring Kelly to and from his magistrates' hearings. We were handcuffed together in the back of a police van and it was on those journeys, to and from court, that was when Kelly told me about all the murders being reported in the media.'

Chapter 7

Captive Audience

What Platt said he witnessed in the police cell before Kelly told him of his other murders matched information provided by Officer A *and* reportage of the trial that was marked on the public record in the British Library. But who else did Kelly kill, according to Platt? What hidden cases were the police tracking down, and the Home Office allegedly trying to cover up?

Platt explained that the answer to those questions was rooted in a series of visits to Wandsworth Prison in 1984. He's not sure if it's still there, but there used to be a hard, wooden seat beside the old gallows in E wing. As a young police constable, he used to rest on that seat and wait for prison staff to escort Kelly up from the cells so he could sign him out.

Between 1878 and 1961, over 135 prisoners had been put to death in Wandsworth Prison. By 1984, the death penalty had been abolished, though as Platt recalls, maintaining the gallows was a routine that staff still followed with grim diligence. He used to hear the release of the trap door and think Kelly was lucky that hanging had been outlawed.

Platt had started going to Wandsworth Prison in late 1983, in the weeks that immediately followed the discovery of William Boyd's body in Clapham Police Station. The former detective said he was drafted in to help with the Kelly case soon after the Irishman was hauled from the cell and arrested for murdering Boyd. He was given the job, among other duties, to collect Kelly from the prison and bring him to court hearings.

Now by Platt's own admission his recall of Kelly's confession – served up in the back of the prison van – was not an orderly one. It was a stream of consciousness that in no particular order listed crime scenes and murder locations including tube stops on the Northern Line, sedate British coastal cities such as Bournemouth, and one of Britain's most infamous incarceration units – Broadmoor.

Some of Kelly's victims didn't have names but monikers, including Scotch Jack, Jock Gordon and Soapy Joe. And according to reports in the press, the murder dates were fluid but on a fixed timeline that ran from 1953 to 1983.

The Kelly murder investigation represented a big break for the then 28-year-old police constable. Up until then, Platt was on the muscle side of the policing business. He had the kind of stature that made him useful when it came to breaking down doors, and his colleagues were happy to have him along on dangerous jobs where they thought they might lose a few teeth.

In the early 1980s, before the murder of Boyd, Platt was known to the vagrants who were part of the landscape of Clapham and its common. He'd collared these petty criminals so often, they knew him by name and he used their nicknames. Convictions for drunkenness, assault, assault with a weapon, theft and aggravated robbery were the commas of common life around Clapham in the 1980s. But the strangulation of William Boyd lit the fuse on a story that exploded into mass murder.

'When the murder happened, we were all drawn in,' said Platt. 'After Kelly's confession, I was sent to the *South London Press* newspaper to look at the archive and old back editions and see what I could find out.' And here, within the newspaper's yellowing musty pages, Platt said he made a startling discovery.

'There were an awful lot of newspapers and flicking through them I found reports of deaths on the Northern Line, of people who jumped,' he said. 'And when I was reading the articles, I discovered that Kelly was reported as a witness to more than one of them.' The archive, he said, corroborated claims Kelly had been making to the young officer when they were cuffed together in the back of the police van. 'That's when I knew he was telling the truth.'

Platt explained that Kelly had been held on remand at both Wandsworth Prison and Brixton Prison while he awaited trial for the murder of Boyd. But it was a feature of his pre-trial that every seven days, Kelly was required to appear in front of a magistrate or district judge. 'It was a major operation,' said Platt. 'Kelly was a Category A prisoner. We'd have to book him out and I'd arrive at Wandsworth Prison every Monday at 9am and sign for him, make sure he was fit and well, and we'd drive to court on blue lights and with the two-tone sirens blaring. Kelly was a violent man and it was my instruction that he was not to share a cell with any other prisoner. Not after what happened with Boyd.

'The governor of Wandsworth Prison had to answer to the Home Secretary in respect of Kelly. It was decided to have one person dealing with Kelly once a week – me!

'I remember this curious incident with a child molester. He was down to appear in court on the same day as Kelly. It took four uniformed police constables to take them both to court. We'd them cuffed together in the van. But Kelly didn't know what he'd done. And all the way to court, they just abused the police.

'I didn't worry about it. I was used to it. We got to court and they were both taken upstairs to be formally introduced. "This man is a suspect in a murder case," we explained about Kelly. "And under no circumstance should they be detained in a cell together. Do you understand?"

'The man cuffed to Kelly was accused of abusing his 4-year-old daughter. He'd held a red-hot iron across her eyes

and blinded her. He'd battered her head against the wall.
Each of them listened to the other's story and they took Kelly
upstairs to do the paperwork. It was the same for the other
prisoner and then they were to be put back in the van together
and taken back to prison. And then on the way back Kelly
erupted:

"'You scum, you child abuser, you don't deserve to live,"
he shouted.

"'WHAT? You murdered sixteen people," yelled the man.

'They fought and they wrestled. Each felt the other man
was the biggest sinner in Britain.

'Kelly wasn't a saint, he knew he was somewhere between
one and 59 million. And he was frantic not to be the worst. He
was a simple character. He was desperate to avoid being the
world's worst sinner and he put himself close to that definition
that he was so keen to avoid.

'Once he was in prison for the rest of his life, it wasn't
a case of just saying sorry. He killed a man in the cells of
a police station and now he's in solitary confinement. It
wasn't safe to give him a knife and fork and put him in with
the general prison population – he'd cut you up into little
pieces.

'Through those weeks, I was the only one Kelly had to talk
to in the entire world. And in the back of the police van as
we drove across London to court – that's when Kelly told me
about all his crimes. And now people are coming forward
with stories about people who they'd thought had committed
suicide on the underground and they think it was Kelly.'

Based on Kelly's testimony and what he'd discovered in old
newspaper archives, Platt said he began piecing together the
timeline now being reported in the media and investigated
by police. 'The murder of William Boyd was the start of the
confession,' he said. 'But the murders started thirty years
before that – in 1953.'

Chapter 8

Coronation Killer

Shop doors opened to a spending spree on 1 June, 1953. Gamages department store in London spilled television sets with bubble-shaped screens, stores such as Fenwick and Bourne & Hollingsworth displayed mannequins dressed in corduroy jackets and from Walthamstow to Westminster, lamp posts dripped red, white and blue bunting. In the pop charts, Frankie Laine sang *I Believe* and on pavements running from Hyde Park Corner to Knightsbridge tube station, people began to gather.

They were there to claim small plots of concrete where they planned to wait until the sun rose on 2 June and then they'd stand on their tiptoes to try and catch a glimpse of Queen Elizabeth II, whose coming coronation had been driving the sales of those television sets.

Significantly, in the days before the coronation, a ship reputedly left Dublin and docked in Liverpool. Among the passengers that disembarked were two men in their early 20s. The men had come to celebrate the coronation and they boarded a train, most probably from Liverpool's Lime Street Station, to London Euston.

Kieran Kelly and Christy Smith had sought out accommodation as close as they could to Westminster Abbey, where the ceremony was taking place. But because of demand they had to settle on a couple of beds beyond the city limits, around the Clapham and Balham area of south-west London.

In Platt's version of events, he doesn't know if the men witnessed the coronation, only that it rained hard on the afternoon of 2 June, and that Kelly and Smith had run to Baker Street Station in central London, where they skipped down the steps under a canopy of umbrellas and were carried by the crowd to the platform. Tube trains swept in and out of the station and the two friends waited behind the safety of the yellow line for their connection to arrive. Kelly had told him so on their journeys in the back of the prison van.

'Then, out of the blue,' explained Platt, 'Smith says: "Hey Kelly, isn't it about time you got married?"' This apparently innocent question set in motion a fatal chain of events. Because Kelly, according to the former detective, was at that time desperately struggling to come to terms with who he was as a person.

'Upon hearing this, Kelly panicked,' said Platt.

'Why?' I asked.

Platt explained how, on one of their journeys to the magistrates' hearings, Kelly had opened up to him about his childhood and the difficulty he'd had in coming to terms with his sexuality. 'Kelly was a repressed homosexual,' said the former detective. 'Since he was a boy he struggled with his sexuality. He'd grown up in a deeply conservative, religious society in Ireland. He'd tried his best to hide his sexuality from his parents and keep it a secret, and all of a sudden Smith is asking him why isn't he married.

'He thought his secret was out,' continued Platt. 'Smith saying that to him meant *he* knew Kelly was gay. I mean, Kelly had been told from a very young age that it was a sin to be a homosexual. He was terrified of the word. It was the worst sin and he hid it to protect himself. He'd bring porn home and stash it on his sock shelf but in a way that his mother could find it. So when he heard what Christy Smith was suggesting, he thought he was doomed.

'He knew that Smith knew people he went to school with, the people down the pub. And if Smith went back to Dublin and said: "Hey, you know that Nosey Kelly is a homo?" Well, that would be the end of his life. He'd lose everything and the end of the world would be upon him. So when Smith makes that comment, Kelly thinks to himself: "He knows my deepest, darkest secret."'

Christy Smith couldn't have read the signals, but Kelly's mind was a chaotic whizz of distressed thoughts, according to Platt. As his panic rose, Kelly saw the solution emerging into Baker Street Station. And with everyone on the platform looking in the direction of the oncoming train, Kelly positioned himself behind Smith. With the train bearing down on them, Kelly shoved his friend clear of the platform to his death.

'Kelly despaired at what he'd done,' shrugged Platt. 'He was sure he'd be picked up by the police. But he wasn't. He just went back to Ireland and told people that Christy Smith had decided to stay on in London.'

The explanation behind Smith's disappearance had featured widely in the press and most prominently in *The Huffington Post*. And if, as suggested, the murder of Boyd in the cells in 1983 broke open the case, then the story of Christy Smith represented the starting blocks of a murder dash that ran for nearly thirty years. What was certain at this point was that Geoff Platt had a tale with the capacity to draw an audience.

'It sounds like a fascinating story,' said a man who had crossed from his seat on the other side of the room. 'It's great, keep it going,' he added.

'I wrote a book about all these murders,' said Platt, reaching down to unzip his sports bag and pluck out a copy.

Listening as the conversation unfolded between the pair, it was obvious Platt revelled in the publicity his story was generating. This heaped further doubt on to an already erratic account. But the fact the police were investigating, demanded his account should be taken seriously. It would be easy to check the Smith case against police records and the death was more than likely logged in Transport for London's archive for the date of the coronation – 2 June 1953. 'Okay,' said Platt interrupting my thoughts. 'Where were we?'

Chapter 9

A Glimpse of Fisher

According to Platt, Kelly didn't set off on a killing spree immediately after he'd murdered Christy Smith at Baker Street Underground Station in 1953. There was a long gap between Smith and the next victim because first and foremost, Kelly was a hopeless, petty criminal. A small-time thief. And he got tangled up in a litany of low-level crime when he returned to Dublin after the Queen's coronation. House break-ins, petty larceny, shoplifting, that kind of thing.

Ironically, according to the former detective, Kelly's crime habit was broken by a move *back* to London, where he got married sometime in the early 1960s.

'Married! But I thought he was a homosexual?' I asked.

'He yearned for the security of family life and needed the cover of a family,' said Platt. 'So when he came back to London he got married. He was 31 and had two children in quick succession. The woman he married, she already had a home *and* five children and Kelly had two more with her. Then, after two years, his wife said she was leaving him and getting back with her first husband who'd just gotten out of prison. Kelly came home one day and found the entire family had moved out.'

According to Platt, this dramatic change in Kelly's personal circumstances hastened his descent into darkness. Without the structure and security family life had given him, he returned to his criminal ways and eventually ended up with a three-year prison sentence for aggravated robbery. He was sent to Broadmoor, known for incarcerating the criminally insane. 'But then *they* said he was sane,' said Platt. 'So he was released.'

However, the way the former detective told it, the crime that ended with Kelly being locked up in Broadmoor was a hugely significant moment because he had again demonstrated a propensity for violence for violence's sake. 'After a couple of months, when he came out of Broadmoor, he started pushing people under trains until he was apprehended and brought to justice,' said Platt.

He explained that Kelly had become fixated with trains because he wanted to experience the rush of adrenalin that had surged through his body when he pushed Smith on to the rail lines at Baker Street Station. But he didn't just push people under trains, Kelly murdered by other means.

'Kelly didn't like homosexuals,' said Platt. 'And any man that made an advance, he'd encourage that, and then use a broken bottle to kill the man and that was that. But the problem for investigators was that Kelly would start to talk about a Monday when it was a Wednesday. Things were muddled in his mind. There were different dates identified and periods and we had to go and look at admissions and then consider them across a whole period. It was difficult to make sense of what he gave us. But one connection was Fisher – the murder he was convicted of, found guilty of by a jury in the Old Bailey and was given a life sentence for.'

Along with William Boyd, the Hector Fisher case was the only other killing Kelly had been tried for and convicted of. Officer A had confirmed that the beating and stabbing to death of a Mr Fisher on Clapham Common in 1975 formed one half of the Irishman's official body count, and the Fisher case had featured in papers of record including *The Times* and *The Daily Telegraph*, though somewhat curiously, not all that prominently.

But Fisher represented something of an anchor in an investigation that was drifting into waters made ever murkier by the murder claims made by the former policeman. 'Fisher got divorced late in life,' alleged Platt. 'He had his own printing company and lived in Clapham, but his business was running down, he started drinking more and got depressed. He had some savings and he used to enjoy a drink to forget his problems and he came into contact with Kelly. They'd drink together.'

According to the former policeman, it was inevitable that Kelly's volatility would cause problems for the failing businessman. 'They went to an off-licence in Clapham. Kelly put the bottles on the counter and Fisher put his hand in his pocket to pay for them. When the guy added up the money, Fisher was 2p short. There was an argument and Kelly tried to bully the shopkeeper, saying he'd return the bottles and make up the difference. The guy said no and didn't want any trouble. But there was friction.'

After leaving the off-licence, Platt said both men walked to a bench close to Holy Trinity church on the nearby common, but the touch paper of Kelly's temper had been lit by the exchange in the shop. It brought on a brutally violent attack.

'He beat him around the head and then decided he was a dirty bugger and started to stab him with a broken bottle and desecrated his privates.'

'Desecrated?' I asked.

'He chopped them up,' said Platt matter-of-factly and explained that Kelly fled, leaving Fisher's badly beaten body slumped on the bench in the darkness. 'The following morning the body was found and no one knew what happened. There were no witnesses. The police investigated, they took statements, but the investigation went nowhere.

'Then, eight years later, after the murder of Boyd in '83, Kelly confessed to the murder. Old files were drawn out and it turns out that Kelly knows details only the killer would know.

He had actually called himself Keith Kelly during the original investigations, but the statements tied in with 1975 and the forensic evidence, and it all fitted together neatly.'

However, when the then 28-year-old constable and his colleagues started trying to piece together Kelly's confession of murder, they quickly concluded that, despite what seemed like cast-iron evidence, the killer was an unreliable witness to his own crime against Fisher. He was also inconsistent in terms of the date and time of the murder.

Investigators also discovered that Kelly had something of a pattern of case acquittals. 'Before the Kelly case, the record of acquittals at the Old Bailey was four,' said Platt, blowing the memory dust off another old case. 'That record belonged to Fred Foreman, one of the Krays' henchmen. He was acquitted of four murders and later, a guy called Thatcher, from Clapham, who committed a murder at Harvey's Wine Bar in Streatham and had had a couple of fights at Newpark Road, *he* was acquitted. Then Kelly comes along and was acquitted again and again and again.'

Platt highlighted an acquittal that followed a murder he said Kelly committed in London's Soho in 1977. Soho then was The Marquee Club, punk venues such as the Vortex, The Coach and Horses pub and stale-looking strip clubs with tired neon lights. Celebrities drank half pints in The French House while winos sat about on pavements outside, trying to score spare change. There was violence. But even by Soho's standards, the murder of Maurice Weighly was disturbing. Weighly was described as another homeless alcoholic whose badly assaulted body was discovered in one of the postcode's alleyways. His genitals had been mutilated and the neck of a broken glass bottle had been thrust up his rectum.

Kelly had denied the murder and in 2015, following the release of Platt's book, the *Daily Star Sunday* reported that he'd been acquitted. But Platt claimed that the Irishman had owned up to the crime.

Platt said Kelly got off again at the Old Bailey in 1982 for the murder of a man, who he claimed had been pushed under a train at Tooting Bec Station. 'Kelly was acquitted for the murder of a Mr Francis that was witnessed by a doctor, a solicitor, and an accountant,' he said. 'They had wrestled Kelly to the ground and held him there and that's not something a doctor would usually do.

'Like Christy Smith, nearly thirty years before, Kieran Kelly unleashed his rage on an innocent commuter who had been stood waiting on the station platform. He pushed Mr Francis under a train. The case went to court and it fell down when the barrister said: "Kelly is someone who pees in bushes – a homeless tramp. How did he know Mr Francis? Why would Kelly want to kill him and why did he upset him?"

'The prosecution had no answer to that. But for reasons we struggled to understand, Kelly saw Mr Francis as being unpleasant and wanted to rid the world of his presence. I mean, if you killed all these people already, then you don't need an excuse to kill the next one.'

In the dining room of the hotel, Platt paused as a waitress approached. 'So sorry,' she said. 'Did you get dessert?' By now, we had moved from the lounge off the reception to the dining room where the steel lids on metal bains-marie clanged and crashed to the tune of the £5 buffet. The waitress was dressed in a black pinafore with a small white apron and held a bowl of chocolate profiteroles. 'Would you like cream?' she asked. 'I'm slim and I can take it,' replied Platt, stretching his arms behind his head. She started to pour the cream, then cast her gaze on the microphone boom resting on the table. 'Are you doing an interview?' she asked. Platt smiled. 'Oh, I bring people here from English TV and Irish radio all the time,' he said.

I thought again of the exchange an hour earlier with the stranger in the hotel reception and how escalating interest in the Kelly story had brought about an almost concurrent increase in Kelly's kill rate which, according to Platt, now stood at thirty-one. This had become a murder story with two disparate ends – the two killings Kieran Kelly was convicted of, and that disorderly whizz of twenty-nine additional murder claims made by the former policeman. But where did the truth lie?

Chapter 10

A Matter of Accuracy

On the train back to London, I started to skip randomly through the three hours of taped recordings I'd just made and apply some order to Platt's version of events. His first count of twelve murders sounded ambitious, never mind his newly revised figure of thirty-one. But more than thirty years on, what was the truth behind a case that led to a commitment to investigate from Britain's top policeman, Sir Bernard Hogan-Howe?

I decided to call the *South London Press*, the newspaper whose archive Platt claimed helped widen the case into a mass murder inquiry in 1983. I explained why I was calling; how a former constable with the Metropolitan Police said the paper's archive led him to expose a killer who stalked the London Underground. In the summer of 2015, the *South London Press* was just one more publication that had run a report on Platt's story of murder and cover-up. But the editor apologized and explained that the newspaper's archive didn't date back to the period in question. If Platt had used an archive, then it no longer existed as a physical record.

I called the Transport for London press office, responsible for all media queries related to the underground. They explained that they couldn't give any information related to deaths on the network and, anyway, they wouldn't have access to information that dated back to the 1950s. It was the same story with the court services, who said they were unable to offer access to a digital record of the Kelly murder trials because they'd yet to be digitized.

There was a reply from the Home Office, however. I'd been calling for a reaction to the allegations of a cover-up since the story emerged. But the emailed response was in keeping with the minuscule thread of information that was starting to typify the case: 'Following on from our conversation, you will need to speak to the police about the allegations of cover-up I'm afraid, as they would be the organisation that investigates.'

The Kelly case was without the kind of administrative footprint that could help substantiate or refute Platt's claims. It seemed as though the only readily accessible physical record lay in the hands of the source, Officer A. 'His memory is not as accurate as it should be,' he said of Platt.

After the dead ends of the *South London Press*, the British Transport Police and the Home Office, I'd called Officer A and explained how it was proving very difficult to get an orderly account of the Kelly case from the self-appointed star witness. And the integrity of Platt, and his story, was again called into question.

'I was thirty years in the Met, dealing with major inquiries, and I never came across Mr Platt,' said Officer A. 'But I've looked into his history and here's the thing – he's not wrong when he says he received a commendation for this work on the Kelly case. It's on his file. *And* in respect of some of his confrontations as an officer, he was attached to a gun unit.

'But it was a different time in the police then. Officers weren't bound to one duty and he may have helped the gun unit at times but there is nothing in his record to say he ever discharged a gun. He never made the rank of detective either. He was a plain clothes police officer.'

The disclosure that Platt had never made the rank of detective further undermined his credibility, but the veracity of his account was proving difficult to challenge due to a lack of evidence. I asked if any other officer was familiar with the name Christy Smith, whom Platt claimed was Kelly's first victim at Baker Street Underground Station.

'Smith! Yeah,' he sighed. 'The file says that in 1983, Kelly *himself* told investigating officers that he murdered a Christy Smith. But we can find no evidence of this. Kelly said he committed the murder and went back to digs. There have been extensive enquiries and we've failed to resolve that case. But again, it was never clear what station this took place at. And the thing about Christy Smith is that there's no evidence to suggest a Christy Smith ever existed.'

Smith was the starting point on Kelly's timeline of murder, according to case expert Platt. I wondered if it was possible that Kelly, or Platt, had got the tube stations mixed up and asked whether the source had ever come across a Mr Francis, who'd apparently been pushed to his death at Tooting Bec Underground Station? 'Oh yes,' he said. 'The Mr Francis he mentioned to you is actually a man called Francis Taylor and he was a friend of Kelly's. Kelly pushed him from a platform in Tooting Bec in 1982. He was charged but later the charge was dropped.'

'So Geoff Platt just got the name wrong?' I asked.

'Yeah, that and the fact that Taylor, well…Taylor survived.'

In direct contradiction to the former policeman's account, the source explained that, by some miracle, Francis Taylor cheated death when he was pushed on to rail lines at Tooting Bec after landing in a shallow well below the rail tracks. Kelly *had* pushed him and this attack *did* occur at Tooting Bec Station, but there was no body and no attempted intervention by any doctors or lawyers, just a sorry squabble between two men who had retreated into the depths of the underground in winter to journey up and down the rail lines for warmth.

Taylor and Kelly were friends and because of some so-called 'code of the common', by the time the trial rolled around, Taylor decided he wanted to drop the attempted murder charge against his friend and the case was acquitted. It was, said Officer A, almost identical to another incident involving Kelly.

'I'm not sure if he mentioned this one to you but it's been reported in the media – an attack on a man known as Jock Gordon.' Like Taylor, Gordon was a sometime drinker on the common. He too had become embroiled in a platform altercation with Kelly but this time at Oval tube station, where Kelly ended up pushing him on to the tracks. He also cheated death because he ended up falling into the service well beneath the rail lines.

'Let me see, let me see, let me see,' muttered Officer A. I could hear him rifling through his files over the phone.

'YES,' he declared loudly.

'PUSHED MALE ON TO RAILS BUT MALE RESCUED BY OFF-DUTY TUBE WORKER.'

'This was from the *Daily Star*…emm, what does it say now? Blah blah blah, Kelly told his solicitor he pushed Jock Gordon on to the railway lines at Oval, blah blah blah, oh, enquiries identified Gordon as GORDON McMURRAY. McMurray was located and he stated that he could identify the person who pushed him. An ID parade was performed and McMurray positively identified Kelly.'

He continued reading: 'This incident was not reported and enquiries to trace the employee who helped him proved negative. Submissions had been put forward to charge Kelly with attempted murder.'

'Listen,' he said. 'I know the investigation is checking if there is a chunk of murders outstanding on the underground and so far, we can find no evidence that there is. What we know for certain right now is that Kelly killed two people: William Boyd and Hector Fisher, and he was sent to prison for life. But neither of them were on the underground.

'The McMurray attack in Oval, that happened. And Kelly was acquitted on the attempted murder charge related to

Francis Taylor, but both men survived. There was another murder charge he was acquitted of – the manslaughter of a man called Edward Toal, who was strangled to death at Kennington Park in 1977. But you are going to have to go through the proper channels in relation to that one.

'What we don't know for certain is the possibilities around some of the other cases Kelly is being linked with. There are some serious crimes there and that's what we are looking into right now. I can't give you details on those cases at the minute, other than there's twenty-four of them.'

It was a surprise to learn that in spite of deep concerns among investigators about Platt's account and his credibility as a witness, police were revisiting a glut of serious crimes linked with Kieran Kelly. 'It's not my place to start giving up information on those cases right now,' he said. 'This isn't my investigation.'

I asked if it was worth filing a Freedom of Information request. 'It wouldn't go anywhere,' Officer A replied. 'The case is a matter of personal, not public, interest, and there is no onus on the authorities to comply.'

But despite this assertion, public interest in the case was mounting, driven by recorded murders, manslaughter, acquittals for attempted murder and confessions of murder the police force never pursued. 'I'll give you a flavour of some of his other crimes outside those twenty-four cases,' said the source, offering to read from the file.

'On 7 February, 1953 in Dublin District Court, he was sentenced to two years' probation for stealing.

'In 1956, in Dublin Circuit Court, he was convicted of housebreaking and sentenced to hard labour for nine months.

'In 1957 in Dublin, he was given two years' hard labour for stealing, shopbreaking and housebreaking.

'1958, court in Dublin and '59, Dublin.

''59 Dublin, '59 Dublin again, '59 Central Criminal Court Dublin...he appears in Dublin a lot.

'He must have come out around 1960 and his next conviction is in '65 in Lambeth for assaulting a police officer.

''66 drunk, '66 damage, '66 theft, '67 theft, '67 possession of tablets, '67 housebreaking, '68 forgery, '68 damage, '68 drunk, '68 drunk and damage, '69 officebreaking, '69 robbery and he was sent to Broadmoor, the home of the criminally insane.

'He is down as being born in Dublin and he came to England in '54. That's his first entry on the police file, even though he says he committed a murder in '53. I've given you his rap sheet up to 1969 and Broadmoor, but Kelly gets out of Broadmoor in '71 and in '72 he assaults a police officer.

'Then, there's a list of offences: '72 damage, '75 threatening behaviour, '75 property damage, '77 shoplifting, '77 burglary, '79 theft, '79 theft, '80 robbery and three years in prison, '82 theft of ten pints of milk, 1982 criminal damage. As you can see, Kelly was in and out of prison most of his adult life. But he was also married – to an Esther Haggins, it says here. And he worked for Richardson's, a building contractors in London.

'Waldegrave Road in Crystal Palace is listed as a former address – that was before he embarked on a life of crime that continues to tie up resources. But listen, right now you are going to have to email in whatever other questions you have and I'll see if I can follow them up.'

This follow-up had two contrasting versions of the truth. One actively promoted in the press by former policeman Platt who, despite the challenges posed by his testimony, had received a commendation for his work on the case. The other, by a well-placed source with access to some of the case notes who, unlike the publicity-hungry policeman, wished to remain anonymous.

The source had no personal stake in the story, other than a cautious willingness to help set the record straight. So it seemed. But while his account cast serious doubt over unsolved murders on the underground and elsewhere, Kelly remained a convicted double killer with a book of twenty-four crimes still being pursued by investigators. Despite the differing accounts, the debunked detective Platt had still posed a question the police didn't yet have an answer to. Just how many people did Kieran Kelly kill?

Chapter 11

Waldegrave Road

The answer to that question was almost certainly not going to emerge from behind the door of one of Kelly's former addresses, but the street named by the source was one I was familiar with. Waldegrave Road was in Crystal Palace and I lived in the same postcode. In recent weeks I'd passed Waldegrave Road, unaware the street was once the home of the man whose story I was chasing. It was the longest of long shots that whoever lived there might know anything about the building's former occupant, but it wasn't impossible. Maybe the person who moved in after Kelly was still living there.

On this summer's evening, whoever lived there had pulled the windows open all the way to let the air in. The afternoon temperature had boiled and then cooled into the kind of evening that pulled tie knots loose, and cars idled by with windows down. On adjacent Anerley Road, red buses streamed by in opposite directions towards Beckenham and Streatham. The urban setting was unremarkable but for the fact that the address was once the home of a convicted double killer and allegedly, one of Britain's most prolific serial killers.

An Asian woman holding a baby opened the door and then a man quickly appeared. 'What's this about?' he asked. I explained that I was looking for information on someone who once lived in the house who was now the centre of a police investigation into cold case crimes. Only, no one seemed to have heard of Kieran Kelly. Had they?

'No, no, no, no,' said the man. 'A serial killer, living here? No, no, I'm sorry. Don't mention that when my girlfriend comes, otherwise she'll go crazy. Listen, we can't help, I'm very sorry.'

The reaction underscored the fact that Kelly and his crimes didn't figure in the public consciousness. No one remembered Kelly in London's Irish community. And no one in authority would comment on the case because they said it was a 'live investigation'. The only person talking openly was Platt. And his counterpoint was the source, Officer A, who refused to meet me and protected his identity behind a veil of anonymity. Like his first alleged victim, Christy Smith, I was beginning to wonder if Kieran Kelly, the killer, ever existed.

Chapter 12

Scratching the Surface

'Kelly was born in Rathdowney, County Laois, in 1928. By the time he came to the attention of cops in London as an adult he was homeless and alcoholic, and possessed a pathological hatred of homosexuals.'

Daily Mail, 2016

In the village square in Rathdowney, County Laois, crows sang from the telephone lines and an articulated lorry rumbled by with its air brakes hissing loud gasps before accelerating away, past fields that sweated the dust exhaled by combine harvesters. It was scorching hot and save for crows and the traffic, the village at the centre of these salacious tabloid stories was deathly quiet.

Situated in the Irish midlands, Rathdowney was the reported birthplace of Kieran Kelly. It was suggested that he'd left more than seventy years before, but despite the passing of time, maybe someone remembered him here. In the village square, I stopped a passer-by and showed him a 2015 news report related to the case. Did the name Kieran Kelly mean anything to him?

'The London Underground serial killer,' said the man, tilting his head to read the bold typeface on the printout. 'Oh yeah, I heard about that,' he said, taking a step back and fixing his hand visor-like above his eyes to block the sun. 'Wait and see now, who would know about that now? Emm, ehh... .' He looked anxiously about the square. 'It was shocking when we heard about it,' he continued. 'But someone said it was a lie. Eh, let's see now, come down here to O'Malley's.' He pointed and then took off down the hill towards the bottom of the square.

The old wooden door of O'Malley's pub had been wedged open. Inside, less than a handful of customers sought cover from the sun in the cool shade of the bar. Light streamed through the open front door and the pint bottles of cider lined up on the counter sweated tiny drops of condensation. At the back, a lean, middle-aged barman was in conversation with a customer.

'Hold on there a second,' said the man from the street, instructing me to wait as he walked down and whispered something in the barman's ear. 'Jesus Christ,' whispered the barman in a barely audible tone. He looked over the man's shoulder towards the door. 'What's this for?' he asked, raising his voice and slinging his white hand towel on to the counter.

He sat up on a high stool. 'I think there still might be family of that man living here,' he said as I walked down. 'I thought there was anyway, but you'd be frightened to check. Who are you meeting?' I explained that I'd made contact with the local historian, Michael Creagh. 'He'd be the right man to talk to,' said the barman, tapping the counter by way of endorsement. 'But Jesus,' he gasped, 'I don't know if there's anyone alive who would have known him. To the best of my knowledge,' he added, contradicting his earlier comment about Kelly still having family here, 'there are no relatives here that are still alive now.'

I asked if the Kelly story had been talked about in the pub. 'Oh, it was huge, AB-SO-LUTE-LY,' he said, pronouncing each syllable separately for effect. 'A serial killer! From Rathdowney? JESUS! There was talk in the bar for weeks and lads remembering snippets and wild stories and that. When it broke in the papers, no one had ever heard anything about it.

That was the first time. There were some Kellys in the town and you were frightened to ask if it was true.

'There was a Byrne man from here who played for Man United and Ireland. He was born in one of the houses up there,' he said pointing out the door. 'He was a friend of my father's. He was the most famous person to come out of the place, and to be associated with a serial killer isn't great. But most people don't have an iota of Kelly. They don't remember his family or him. This book that the policeman wrote, that was the first of it.

'Listen,' he said, standing up off the high stool and whipping the white hand towel from the counter. 'Michael Creagh will be able to help you.'

I walked back up towards the village square to meet Michael Creagh. Less than an hour in Rathdowney and it seemed certain that this quiet, sedate village was the hometown of the same Kieran Kelly that had made headlines around the world. And his story had captured the imagination of locals. I had time before Michael Creagh arrived so I walked up towards the village supermarket where a scatter of cars were parked in the shade. In the driver's seat of one, a man saluted a breezy wave. I walked over and explained I was trying to find information on the so-called London Underground serial killer – Kieran Kelly.

'Kieran Kelly,' he blurted. 'Yeahhhh...the serial killer, in London,' he added, shifting his body to sit more upright in the seat. 'I'll tell you if you go out here, take a right and go up the road there,' he pointed, 'there's a row of cottages and there's an old boy who lives up there. Normally, he sits outside on days like this...worked in London I think...has a patch over the eye...Mark Whelan is his name. He might be able to help you. He'd be old enough I'd say to have known him. If *he* doesn't know, then I don't know who would.'

The man nodded in the general direction of the house as if to reinforce his instructions, then turned the key in the engine of the car. 'But come here,' he said loudly before driving away. 'Is the story true like?'

Chapter 13

Tube Interchange

'Serienkiller tötete U-Bahn-Pendler in London von Caroline Freigang – In den Siebzigern geisterte ein Serienkiller durch die U-Bahn-Schächte Londons. Die Behörden vertuschten die Sache. Jetzt packt ein Polizist aus.'

20 Minuten newspaper, Switzerland

Allegations that the Kelly story of mass murder was true were now making headlines in Europe, as well as England and the US, and the proposed crime scene was one the man with the patch over his eye, Mark Whelan, was more than familiar with. Whelan used to stand in the half light of Neasden Depot in north-west London and watch the headlights of trains limping towards the maintenance sheds from central London.

Neasden Depot was a pit stop on the Metropolitan Line of the London Underground. The carriages used to groan and screech as they wobbled into the sidings after long shifts running the city's rail network red hot. Neasden felt solemn on those mornings, before sunrise shattered a dark sky illuminated by orange street lamps.

It was Mark Whelan's job to clean the trains when they arrived. Old newspapers. Food wrappers. Cigarette butts. Sometimes, he'd find homeless people asleep or bleary-eyed passengers trying to figure out where they were after waking up to discover they'd missed their stop. Very occasionally, a train would limp into the depot after colliding with a person and Whelan might spot some blood, or worse, a body part in the tangle of cogs and springs. He never figured on anyone being pushed to their death on a tube line. Or that a man, a former neighbour of his, would eventually make headlines around the world for murder.

'I knew his father,' said Whelan, clearing his throat. 'Martin Kelly, that was his father's name and he lived up the Ballybuggy Road there.' He waved his hand. 'He had a sister, this chap you talk about, and they had a shop and it was a hut more than a building and it was right in front of John Ahern's at Enda O'Reilly's pub and he, Martin Kelly, used to sell sweets. Later, it became a barber shop.'

These memories represented the first confirmation from a non-authority figure that a Kieran Kelly, convicted of murder in London, both existed and came from Rathdowney. And the strange thing about the person confirming that fact was that Mark Whelan once worked on the underground network, upon which his neighbour claimed to have committed multiple murders. Thin and dressed in a pair of neat-fitting slacks and a light-coloured shirt with a breast pocket, Whelan said he remembered the Kelly family from growing up in the village in the 1930s.

'Do you remember what type of man the father was?' asked the historian Michael Creagh, who had collected me from the village square after the conversation with the man in the parked car. 'I didn't take much notice of him,' replied Whelan. 'I knew him as a tall man. He'd dark hair and a chiselled face.'

'The picture we've seen of Kieran was like that,' said Creagh. 'He'd an angular face with a long nose?' Whelan nodded.

'That's it exactly. I was probably 10 or 11 then when they had the shop. Later, I remember it going around Rathdowney that his son killed someone in England. I was home on holiday when I heard. But is it true?'

Whelan listened intently as he was told that Kelly was convicted and sentenced to life in prison for two killings. But he had confessed to committing dozens more murders and, following the disclosures of a former policeman, his historical confession was currently under investigation by British police.

'BY JOVE,' he said. 'I thought it was just one he did.'

'The first murder Kelly said he did was in Baker Street,' I added.

'Oh, we did get trains from Baker Street,' observed Whelan. 'And we used to get a steam engine in there as well, but I have lost most of my memory.'

'Is there anything you remember about the Kellys?' Creagh pressed.

Whelan took a moment to think as commentary from a horse race, somewhere in England, leaked from a television set in the corner. 'It must have been the spring,' he said after a while. 'There was a gang of us. I'm not sure whether Kieran Kelly was there but he'd one sister, Edith Kelly I think was her name. She was a real tearaway. We'd be up in the moor at the back of Nicky Meagher's house. It was a wild place, and we found a bird's nest and she killed the birds with a penknife, and I always thought it was very cruel.'

Behind Whelan's glazed-over eyes, a decades-old memory of an innocent childhood adventure was replayed, since and forever tainted by the senseless spilling of blood in the springing of the year. Rousing himself from the recollection, he added: 'That's all I can remember about the Kellys really.'

Chapter 14

School Ties

If Mark Whelan couldn't remember anything else worthy of recall then he had a neighbour of similar years who had vivid memories of Kelly. Only Mick Ryan wasn't keen on sharing them. 'I don't want to speak out of turn, d'ye know wha' I mean?' he said in a thick accent. 'I don't want to be saying anything against the Kellys,' he added defiantly. 'Ye know wha' I mean?'

It was late afternoon in a small cottage on the outskirts of Rathdowney. The setting sun had dimmed the light in the house and Mick Ryan was getting agitated. Now in his late eighties, he had lived in the village of Rathdowney all his life and had once known the Kellys well – very well in fact. This was why he didn't want to talk ill of Kieran, who he once went to school with.

He wasn't convinced by the explanation that the purpose of the conversation wasn't to illicit a negative image of Kelly, just to try and untangle the truth behind his story, and the disparity of his killing tally of two, and thirty-one.

'OK,' he said sharply, after taking a moment to think. 'I remember it was around the time of the Spanish Civil War, that's how far back ye're going, ye know what I mean? It was 1936 and we were going to national school in Rathdowney.' He explained that, at the time, Irishmen were in the process of joining up with the international brigades and shipping out to Spain to fight in the civil war. They learned about the conflict through their teachers, the Christian Brothers, who knew Irishmen, on both sides, that went to fight in the conflict. He remembers talking about the war with his neighbour, Mick Brophy. They were in the same class and around the same age, but Ryan looked up to Brophy and sought guidance from him. He wasn't the only one.

There was a small, quiet boy with light-coloured hair who used to walk alongside them to school. His name was Kieran Kelly and he lived with his parents and sister on a winding lane, just outside the village – the Ballybuggy Road. Ryan didn't then understand qualities such as self-assurance and insecurity. But he could see the former quality in the confident Brophy and the latter in the uncertain Kelly.

'He was insecure,' said Ryan. 'He wouldn't have been as up-to-date as the rest of us, and he wouldn't have been as up-to-date as Mick Brophy, that's for sure,' he frowned. 'He was a bit gawpy,' he explained. 'Yeah, he relied on Mick Brophy, who was a caring type of a guy, a fella who was ahead of his time, really.'

Ryan explained how Brophy would often have to give Kelly reassurance after school, just at the point when they were all breaking off to go home. 'He'd tell him not to worry about school, that everything would be OK the next day,' said Ryan. 'To be honest with you,' he followed, 'it's all from the early years because the family must have left town when he was around 10 years old, I reckon.'

If Mick Ryan was right and the family had left the town when Kelly was 10, that would have made it some time in the 1940s – seventy years ago. But an enduring image remained of an uncertain young boy, from a seemingly stable family, who grew up on a quiet lane before moving away, and eventually ended up in prison in London. And part of the reason Mick Ryan remembers him is that he was given cause to reflect on the Kellys by something that happened in 1984. 'That was the next time I heard of Kieran Kelly,' he said. 'It was yearrrrs later, when a man, Tom Butler, came around with the *Evening Herald* newspaper. And there he was in it, Kieran Kelly, for a trial in London.'

Chapter 15

The Dig

Long before Kelly's Old Bailey trial was reported in the *Evening Herald* in 1984, Nicky Meagher used to stretch out his arms as far as he could and lean into the crowd. It was all he could do to try and hold back the evening rush of commuters. Every day, thousands of them spilled down the stairs from Euston Road and deep into the bowels of King's Cross tube station in London. They'd be packed tight along the stairs and down the length of the station's old wooden escalators. It was chaotic and energizing.

In the 1950s, Meagher worked as a platform attendant for London Underground. The Northern, Piccadilly, Victoria, Circle, Hammersmith and City and Metropolitan Lines of the network all ran through and dumped out passengers at the enormous hub of King's Cross. More than 150 metres below a tangle of streets that leaked into Camden in the north, Euston to the west and south towards the West End, shockwaves of people pulsed in and out of the capital from the station exits.

King's Cross was also a mainline station servicing the north of England and cities such as Bedford and Leicester. Workers poured on to the station's platforms from these commuter towns and it was Meagher's job to keep them moving. From County Laois and of medium height and build, Nicky Meagher had only got the job of platform attendant by chance.

He had tramped the city looking for work, growing lean from all the walking and weary from all the asking. But there was nothing to be had. In 1956, London was in the midst of a credit squeeze. Without the price of a bus fare, people walked for miles searching for work. 'NOT HIRING' signs hung heavy from gates outside building sites. Then, Meagher stumbled upon a sign that the London Underground was recruiting. Within a week, Meagher's working vocabulary found itself reduced to a couple of safety catchphrases on London's subterranean network. 'Mind the gap please. Watch the doors.'

There were accidents of course. Eager passengers racing to make connections and tumbling down stairs, mainly. Cuts. Bone breaks. Deep gashes. And always the threat that someone might end up on the line. 'I remember one lad died in Angel tube station,' he said, while walking slowly along the Ballybuggy Road in Rathdowney. 'I reckon it was a suicide, and he finished on the far track.

'I remember the bosses saying if someone goes on to the tracks, the first thing to do was run up to the top of a platform, pull a lever, kill the power and then call for assistance. I knew drivers in the canteen who hit people but no one really talked about them, not the suicides. And there were a lot of people, like vagrants, who used the Northern Line in winter. They'd get on at the top of the line and go up and down all day to keep warm. Around King's Cross, there was a toilet and pimps, oh God you'd be afraid to walk down through the place.

'They were rough characters, a lot of Scots, and some of our own lads from Ireland too. But really, I'm not sure how much help I can be to you,' he said. Meagher had slowed his step and come to a stop outside the gated entrance of a small two-storey cottage on the Ballybuggy Road.

Mark Whelan and the local historian, Michael Creagh, had suggested Meagher may be a big help. Because not only did he – like Whelan – once work on the London Underground, he grew up on the same plot of land that was once Kelly's home.

'That's it now,' said Meagher, leaning on the gate in front of the cottage. 'It's a typical labourer's cottage, really,' he added. 'The Kellys moved out in 1937 and we moved in in 1938, I think. There used to be old blue slates on the roof and then a canopy over the porch. When we were growing up there was eleven of us. The boys had one room and the girls had another and there was an outside toilet. I wouldn't know how many children were in the Kelly house; you'd probably have to ask Mark Whelan that.'

It felt like a peculiar happenstance that along with Whelan, Meagher had worked in the same transport network, upon which Kelly had allegedly murdered through the same period. But even more freakish was the fact that Kelly once lived on the site where Meagher lived now, and had done for some years. 'I was born in 1935 and we moved in this house when I was 3,' he said, waving an arm at the cottage. 'Kelly moved out around 1937 and went to Dublin, the *bould* fucker.'

Meagher leaned both arms on the wall of a lane that wound off into deep countryside and started to talk about how this shared experience only became something significant in 1984, following a conversation with a close friend, Ned Kearney. Kearney lived on the opposite side of the road to where Meagher lives now. And because Rathdowney was a small community, you knew your neighbours and what they were up to. Ned Kearney's sister, Daisy, left Ireland in the early 1940s, and having worked in London for many years himself before returning, Meagher was always interested to hear what Daisy was up to. She wrote letters about work. She wrote letters about where she lived. She wrote about people she bumped into from home. People such as Kieran Kelly. 'Daisy knew him as a young lad,' said Nicky. 'She bumped into him in London, knew him and his friends and that he was in trouble a good bit. She knew that as well.

'Come up here,' he said, turning on his toes and walking back towards the entrance to his home. 'In 1984, I was in the front garden there,' he pointed, 'and Ned came across the road. He told me that Kieran Kelly was on trial at the Old Bailey for two murders. That's what Ned said. He said Kelly killed a rake of people in London. The whole town knew about it. It was in the press and there were articles in the English tabloids in 1984. Daisy wrote and told Ned about it too. And then the cop wrote about it years later – that Kelly confessed to all these murders. There was one lad in a park and another in a police station and he stamped on his head because he was snoring. All that information came from Daisy.'

Meagher stopped outside the front entrance to his home and recalled how, not long after Daisy's news, people stopped bringing up Kelly's crimes. The countryside returned to its usual silent, seasonal rhythm until nine years later when it surrendered a dark secret.

'Did I tell you about digging for the water pipe here?' he asked, almost as an afterthought, nodding at a spot on the ground outside his driveway entrance. 'Back in 1993? No? With my son, young Nick?' I shook my head. 'Geez, I thought I'd told you that,' he said, scolding himself.

'Well, it was 1993 and I started digging a shallow trench in the front garden to lay a water pipe. Then I hit something hard and I turned over the sod. And there were bones. Then we dug some more and there were more bones, and a skull, and the skull had a wire noose around the neck.'

A Skull.

Bones.

A wire noose.

In less than thirty seconds, it felt like Nicky Meagher had shot the Kieran Kelly story into a higher stratosphere. This disclosure felt revelatory; a dramatic footnote coming at the tail end of a two-hour conversation. 'What happened then?' I asked. 'Well, suddenly, it came into my head about Kelly,' he said. 'And what Ned Kearney said back in '84. So I rang the Guards and called the local doctor, Niall O'Doherty, and he came up and said that he thought it was human remains. Human, yeah that's what he said.'

Wide-eyed, I asked Meagher if the doctor who witnessed the find, O'Doherty, was still around. 'Oh yeah,' he replied, 'the doctor still lives in the town here.' I asked for the doctor's number, understanding the credibility of this claim demanded a second witness. Then I left Meagher's with an assurance to return and immediately made contact with the doctor. After a brief introduction, he backed up the story and agreed to go on the record at a meeting at the Meagher home later in the week.

* * *

A few days later, retired doctor Niall O'Doherty was sitting on the front wall of the house alongside the owner. 'That's it now,' said Meagher, leaning forward from the wall and nodding at a pillar beside the driveway, underneath which the remains were discovered. 'I dug down about 18 inches,' he said offering a quick revision. 'It was around that depth for a water pipe. Then I found a bone and I went further.

'I called the Gardaí and they sent them over from Templemore. I'm not sure how far they went down, just that when they arrived they told us to stand aside while they had a look. But this is where the remains were found. Niall said it could be human and there was a noose. I thought: "Jesus, someone has got done in here." That's what I thought when I seen the noose around the neck. It was a thickish wire, like a bull wire. You had the skull and the neck and the rest of the bones were loose.'

'The rope was around the skull and under the chin,' O'Doherty chipped in. 'It wasn't a complete body but a collection of bones buried in a mucky hole.'

'At the time I wondered, was it a baby?' stated Meagher. I asked him if it looked suspicious to him. 'Well, the noose around the neck did,' he replied. 'And the fact Kieran Kelly once lived here and that's what put it in my head. Then when they finished, the police said it was a donkey and I said: "It's a small neck for a donkey."'

'If it was the skull of a donkey, it would have a snout,' observed O'Doherty. 'I'm certain it wasn't a donkey,' replied Meagher, his gaze still fixed on the patch of ground at the entrance to his driveway.

'Did you get the Garda records?' O'Doherty turned and asked me. I explained that an attempt to retrieve Garda records was the second phone call I'd made after leaving the Meagher home days earlier; that requests had been made with the regional Gardaí stations in Portlaoise and Abbeyleix to get whatever details they might have on such a call out in 1993. The Gardaí had been made aware that two independent witnesses had confirmed the discovery of bones on a property once home to a convicted killer; a killer now at the centre of a revived murder investigation in Britain. The Garda who took the call logged the details and asked for the specifics of the discovery to be sent via email.

'I made the opinion that it could be human and to get it analyzed,' O'Doherty continued. 'If they felt there was any chance it was human they surely would be back here and say what date the bones were from.'

'The Guards said it would be a good excuse to come to England and interview Kelly,' laughed Meagher. 'And that whoever done it would be long dead.'

'With carbon dating now, they can put the exact date on how long it was there,' reasoned the doctor. 'They found thousands of intact skulls in nearby Cullahill – the children's graveyards.'

'I know where you're talking about,' said Meagher. 'They'd be still so well preserved, the bones could be a long time in a place and look no different. And the Kelly house would have stood alone here and there would have been a lot of shacks around and the remains could have been someone living on the plot here, even before the Kellys.'

'Nicky, are you able to say when the Kelly house was there from?' asked O'Doherty.

'I'd say the 1900s,' he replied. 'This house might have been built over another mud cabin. The number of houses that have disappeared have been many.'

The men stood quiet, looking at the pillar to the entrance of the home Meagher had built on the original Kelly plot, next door to the cottage where both he and the Kelly family once lived. Then, as if to progress the line of tension further, Meagher broke the silence and added yet another layer of intrigue to the story. It chimed with something mentioned by both Mark Whelan and Mick Ryan.

Reflecting on the discovery of bones, he mused: 'I don't know, I just thought it strange that the family disappeared to Dublin all of a sudden and were never seen again.' He paused, as if to allow that thought to settle. Then he recalled how, after the family had left the village, Kelly's mother would return on what sounded like annual pilgrimages to visit her old home.

'I remember my sister Agnes saying that one of the Kellys used to bring the mother back every year to look at the house,' he said. 'Agnes says the mother was anxious and that she never called into the house. They'd just sit in the car outside the house and look at it, but never call in. They'd just say that they'd come to see the house.'

'A lot of families do that, come back and see relations,' reasoned O'Doherty. 'Yeah, but to keep coming back to look at the house, I thought was strange,' replied Meagher.

I listened to the men's discussion and wondered about these strange return visits, how germane they appeared following the discovery of suspected human remains at the one-time home of a convicted double killer. A killer who'd confessed to additional murders. It could have been animal. But why was there a wire noose around its neck? Or was it just a remarkable coincidence? A freak happening with no link whatsoever to the Kelly family?

'The Gardaí should be able to clear it up pretty quickly with DNA testing,' I suggested optimistically. 'Of the bones?' asked Meagher cynically. 'Well, the Guards just took them away in 1993 and that was the last I heard of it.'

Chapter 16

First Confirmation

So far, the list of people who had heard about or claimed to know about Kelly anchored his story.

The debunked 'detective' Geoff Platt.

Officer A.

The people who said they went to school with Kelly, or grew up beside him.

And the physical paper trail was little more than a few newspaper sidebars in the archive of the British Library, until an electronic printer in a modest home outside Rathdowney coughed up a report card with details of Kelly's aforementioned marriage.

'Kieran Kelly, married on May 8, 1961 in Church of Sacred Heart, Camberwell, Southwark, London SE5 to Frances Esther Territt,' read the text.

Camberwell was the right side of London to Waldegrave Road where Kelly had lived, according to Officer A, albeit he had given the surname of Kelly's wife as Haggins, not Territt. And it had been said that the Irish construction worker descended into the depths of a murderous crime spree after this marriage fell apart sometime in the mid-1960s. The details were part of Kelly's parish record, a succinct log surrendered by a computer belonging to the Catholic church in Rathdowney's parochial house, where his date of birth was also logged.

'Born 16/03/1930 in Rathdowney.

'Baptised 21/03/1930 in Rathdowney by Fr P Dunphy CC.

'Godparents, James McDonald and Elizabeth Kavanagh.'

Like much in this case, the date of birth contradicted media reports and Platt's claim that Kelly was born in 1923. But the record did confirm what Mark Whelan, Mick Ryan and Nicky Meagher said – that the family had left Rathdowney before Kelly had hit his teens.

'Kieran Patrick Kelly: Confirmed - 19/02/1942 in St Kevin's Church, Harrington Street, Dublin by Most Reverend Dr. Wall,' read the third entry.

According to his baptismal record, Kelly would have been 12 years old in 1942 and 54 years old when he was convicted, four decades later, in the Old Bailey of two killings.

Following the conversation with Meagher and O'Doherty, retrieved Irish census details recorded an address for the family around the corner from St Kevin's Church, on 43 Harrington Street in Dublin's south inner city. Ironically, number 43 Harrington Street was now the an Gardaí headquarters for murder investigations. And by cross-referencing the church records and parish records, it seemed certain that Kelly's father *was* the Martin Kelly that Mark Whelan had spoken about.

The location of birth for Martin Kelly was given as the nearby town of Mountmellick and the records said he'd married an Annie North, who was born in Dublin in 1900. Annie North was Kieran Kelly's mother – the woman who, in the years after the family moved, reportedly made annual pilgrimages to their one-time home on the Ballybuggy Road in Rathdowney to 'look' at her old house.

Kieran Kelly was listed as having one sister, a Mary E. Kelly, born in 1932. This must have been the girl Mark Whelan was talking about – who killed the birds in the nest. Both Annie North and Mary E. Kelly had death registration dates of 1951 and 1956 respectively. This made it safe to assume that Kelly's immediate family were long dead by the time he was convicted of the two killings in 1984 – William Boyd and Hector Fisher.

But years after his crimes and alleged crimes, the story had a renewed focus in these claims of discovery in the garden of the Kellys' former home in Rathdowney. Was this the reason the Kelly family left town all of a sudden in the late 1940s and settled in Dublin? And did Annie Kelly's reported annual returns, on the same calendar date, mark some kind of anniversary that had some connection with her son, or even a sibling? It was beginning to feel like a peculiarity of the Kelly story that, as a fuller picture emerged, so did a growing body count.

Chapter 17

Through the Roof

On the evening of 22 December 1974, Brian Sliman, a builder from County Roscommon in the west of Ireland, emerged from an apartment complex he was working on in the Victoria area of London. He was trying to finish up in time for Christmas and the streets surrounding the SW1 postcode were cold and dark, save for the speckle of fairy lights that peaked out from behind the curtains of expensive apartments. The builder loaded the few tools he needed for the next day into his van, then turned the key in the engine and pulled out of Victoria, heading south.

He hadn't driven far when he heard a loud explosion coming from the streets behind him. Minutes later he hit a police checkpoint. He wound down the window of his van and listened as officers told him there'd been a bomb attack on the home of the former prime minister, Ted Heath. They wanted to know where he was coming from and the builder explained that he'd been working on an adjacent property. He'd only just left there, minutes before.

It was a tense exchange. He was Irish, it was the mid-1970s when the IRA were active, and he was driving a van from the vicinity of a bomb attack. He'd later tell people that it was almost impossible for the police *not* to consider him a person of interest.

Ted Heath wasn't home at the time of the attack. The former prime minister arrived ten minutes after an IRA unit had detonated a 2lb pipe bomb outside his home. Afterwards, witnesses told police they saw a Ford Cortina – not a builder's van – leaving the scene. But whenever Heath's name popped up in conversation, Brian Sliman would share that story, or another, from an afternoon in 1999 when he was working on a different job, this time in Fulham.

The job was just a couple of doors down the road from where the BBC reporter Jill Dando lived. And this particular day, the popular *Crimewatch* presenter was shot and killed on the doorstep of her home. The builder joked that fate had conspired to place him at the scene of two major crimes that continued to linger in the consciousness of the British public. However, there was a third murder story that the British public knew nothing about – only this time the builder knew the killer personally.

It's a story he still struggles to make sense of. He worked side by side with this man for years and some of the crimes he was accused of – and his reasons for committing them – just didn't sound like the man he once knew. A man who frequented the Irish bars of south London where, typically, mucky boots were lined up along the counter and spikes of laughter punctured the smoky atmosphere.

Brian Sliman recalled a scene littered with punters, pints of Guinness and tankards of Watneys, where the floors were dirtied by the dusty dandruff shed by the men's boots. He had a strong memory of one particular night when a man was standing on a bar stool, waving theatrically. The man was taking off the famous Grand National horse race.

'And as the leaders come to the Canal Turn, it's still Bob Champion and Aldaniti,' the man yelled. He was of average height and build and wore his grey hair combed back across his head. He was reciting, verbatim, historical commentary from the world-famous race that takes place every year at Liverpool's Aintree track.

The man was neatly dressed, despite having worked on a building site that afternoon, and he spoke with a Dublin accent, though back then he was doing a brilliant impersonation of the Irish sports broadcaster, Michael O'Hehir. The man turned up the volume on his race commentary and the drinkers standing at the counter cheered as the names of horses fell from his mouth in a steady spool.

'Royal Mail is over in second,' he said. 'Rubstic is third and Senator Malacury is behind that, and three behind that is Spartan Missile...and as the leaders run up to Valentine's Brook, Aldaniti is over...and Three of Diamonds is gone at the back... .

'It's Aldaniti, then Royal Mail, then Rubstic, then Senator Malacury, then Spartan Missile and Royal Exile... .

'They go to the third last, it's Aldaniti, closely pressed now by Royal Mail...Three to One is in third, fourth place is Senator Malacury...but as they cross the Melling Road, it's Aldaniti, from Royal Mail, Senator Malacury, Three to One, Spartan Missile, Rubstic and Royal Exile.'

As the race closed in on the finish, Sliman recalled how the names of the horses started to tumble out louder at a faster rate.

'ALDANITI JUMPS IT TWO LENGTHS CLEAR OF ROYAL MAIL, SPARTAN MISSILE JUMPS IT THIRD AND IS FINISHING STRONGLY...THEN COMES SENATOR MALACURY AND THREE TO ONE.

'ALDANITI IS BEING PRESSED NOW BY ROYAL MAIL, AND SPARTAN MISSILE IS FINISHING STRONGLY.

'IT'S ALDANITI NOW AS THEY COME TO THE ELBOW.

'THEY'VE GOT OVER A FURLONG TO RUN AND IT'S ALDANITI IN THE LEAD BUT BEING PRESSED NOW BY SPARTAN MISSILE.

'IT'S ALDANITI FROM SPARTAN MISSILE AND HERE COMES JOHN THORN...AND 54-YEAR-OLD JOHN THORN IS PUTTING IN A STORMING FINISH.

'BUT IT'S ALDANITI FROM SPARTAN MISSILE...
ALDANITI IS GOING TO WIN IT...ALDANITI WINS THE
NATIONAL!'

'Well done, Ken!' they would shout from the bar when the
man finished and he would step down off the stool and rejoin
his friends at the counter.

This was typical of the scene the builder heard colleagues
raving about in the late 1970s. But forty years on, he found
himself reflecting more and more on this captivating stage
show, and not just because he was impressed. 'Ken was
brilliant at doing the Grand National,' said Sliman, sitting in a
chair to the rear of The Hop Pole pub in Wandsworth, south-
west London. 'People used to always be on to Ken to do it. I
don't know if it was that exact race, but he could remember
every horse, every fence, the order of the commentary. It was
brilliant. He was very popular. Charismatic. If he was in the
mood, he could come into this bar here now and talk with
anyone.

'We always called him Ken, but his name was Kieran.
Kieran Kelly. And the last I heard of Ken Kelly was back in
the 1980s, when he was convicted of two murders.'

It was a late evening in the pub and a television hanging
on the wall by the bar leaked news headlines. Less than a
handful of punters sat around making conversation, oblivious
to the significance of information that had been disclosed at
the rear of the premises. I'd spent months hammering contacts
in London's Irish community, searching for someone, anyone,
who might know of, or had even heard of, Kieran Kelly.
From long-serving publicans in some of the city's landmark
Irish bars, to senior figures working in outreach services with
emigrant support agencies. Only no one in the emigrant Irish
community, from which the killer hailed, knew a thing.

Then, unprompted and out of the blue, this builder from
County Roscommon, Brian Sliman, revealed an arm-pinching
connection with Britain's latest supposed serial killer. We'd

only met an hour earlier to discuss him working on a loft conversion in my own home, when the conversation wandered into an old job on Ted Heath's home, Jill Dando's murder and then, a connection of staggering coincidence. It felt like the most remarkable break.

'You knew Kieran Kelly?' I asked.

'Yeah, why?' he wondered. 'Ken, I worked with him.'

'How long?'

'Four years.'

'FOUR YEARS!'

'Why, did you know him?' he asked.

Brian Sliman was surprised to learn that he'd innocently revealed a link that I'd been searching in vain to find. How Kelly's crimes were still under investigation and how, up to now, the profile of the killer was a dark, one-dimensional portrait, painted largely by the authorities' brushstrokes.

The unearthing of the builder felt as remarkable as the skeleton find on the site of the killer's home. Potentially, it was even more important because it was an opportunity to reimagine Kelly, possibly even redefine him. Sliman explained that he had lost touch with Kelly, only to find out years later that his former colleague was convicted of two killings and had been sentenced to life in prison.

'We called him Mad Ken but everyone called him Ken to his face,' he said. 'An ex-policeman, Geoff Platt, started talking about him in the press, saying he killed all these people. But do you think it's true? They said he was gay, but not for a minute would I ever have thought that about Ken. He always had a girlfriend. And all the reports that he was dirty and a tramp – I worked beside him for four years and he was always clean. That's just not true. I have to say, I find a lot of this story hard to believe.'

And from there, Brian Sliman started talking about the first time he'd ever met Kieran Kelly.

* * *

The date, month and exact year escaped him but he was on a job in Balham, south London many years ago and the property, a derelict house, was fenced off with rusting grey sheets of galvanizing. He'd driven into the street and had slowed to find a parking space when he noticed a man in an agitated state pacing about outside the site. He was of average build with longish grey hair.

Sensing something wasn't right, Sliman locked all the doors on the van after he'd parked up. But as he walked towards the site entrance, the man stepped into his path and swung violent punches that crashed into the grey steel of the galvanizing. 'His teeth were gritted,' said Sliman. 'His fist was clenched and he roared at me: "Have you got a job?"'

Startled and anxious to get away, Sliman asked the man if he could fill a skip with rubble from the site. 'It was more to get rid of him than anything. He was punching the galvanizing so hard, I would have thought he'd have broken both his hands. I told him to come back the next day. He just went off and I didn't think about it again.'

The next morning, when the builder parked up, the man was there again, loitering near where he'd pounded his fist into the galvanizing the previous afternoon. Only now, his hair was neatly combed and the air of menace, so potent the day before, had dissipated. 'The first thing he did was apologize for the day before, that he was a bit drunk,' said Sliman. 'It was like he was a different person. And he introduced himself as Ken – Ken Kelly. I mean it was night and day, Jekyll and Hyde stuff.'

Under pressure to get to another job, he left Kelly with instructions to fill the skip outside the property. When he returned later that evening to lock up, he fully expected the skip to be empty. But as he walked towards the house, he spotted a pair of crossed legs stretched out from the doorstep and wisps of cigarette smoke. 'He'd cleared everything from the house, the place was spotless and the skip was neatly loaded to the top. He'd done three or four days' work,' said Sliman. 'And he was just sitting there on a bag of cement, smoking a fag.'

Sliman told the man to come back again the next day, which he did – and the day after that, and the day after that too. 'Ken was a willing worker with a wild streak. But you could never leave him on his own. He'd be gone to the pub. I had a lot of maintenance jobs with the local authority then. It was around 1974/75 and I always brought Ken with me. He was clean and we worked well together. It was like a surgeon doing an operation. Ken always knew exactly what tool I'd need next and he'd be on me shoulder there to hand it to me.

'We'd get through a mountain of work. Then, when the job was done I'd go and deal with the customer and Ken would go down and clean up the van. I'm telling you, the van was absolutely spotless. Ken had everything neatly packed away, right down to the 3cm bolts and screws. We had a box there with everything in it and we started calling it the doctor's bag. He could tell you that we'd eight screws left, or three bolts. He'd have all the paperwork folded neatly in the front of that van. It was later that we started calling him Mad Ken – not because he was insane, just because he did mad things. Like Brixton Hill.'

Brixton Hill is a 1km slope of road that rests between the areas of Brixton and Streatham Hill in south London. According to Sliman, Kelly lived on the hill for a time in the 1970s, in an old house conquered by some property developer and converted into flats. Typically, in the evenings, Kelly used to kick back after dinner, open a bottle of Guinness and watch TV. But on this particular evening there was a knock on the door of Kelly's flat. It was the woman who lived upstairs and she'd called down to collect the rent. 'Kelly himself was shacked up with some woman,' said the builder. 'But on this night his lady was out.'

Kelly handed over the money that was due. But something he was watching on television caught the woman's attention, so she hung on for a bit. There was nothing inappropriate, but the woman's partner arrived home from work to find his lady alone with Kelly in Kelly's flat and the man made accusations of impropriety. 'At the same time, Ken's then-girlfriend came home and she got involved,' said Sliman. 'Ken got drunk and exploded. You could hear their argument from the top of the building apparently. He lost the head and started roaring the building down, calling them niggers and coons.'

The argument escalated. Kelly taunted the woman's partner, racially abusing him *and* other residents who he tried to goad into a fight in the backyard of the building, where he'd hidden an iron bar. 'He was shouting at them all saying: "I'll meet you out the back at high noon,"' said Sliman. 'He went down to the yard in his socks, but none of them would come all the way into the backyard with him. They were wary.'

That wariness eventually subsided and the men did follow Kelly to the backyard, and he attempted to lure them to the corner where he'd hidden the iron bar. The men held their distance but their anger was charging to the point that they'd soon attack. Sensing the danger, Kelly used the darkness to slip away.

At the rear of the yard there was a wall running between the alleyways and gardens on Brixton Hill. Wearing only his socks, Kelly slipped along the tightrope of brick and emerged into the street. Then he snuck back into the building, ran up the stairs and closed the door in his flat. 'They didn't know where he went,' said Sliman. 'The next day I heard from one of the other residents that she was convinced someone was going to be killed down there that night. I later said: "Ken, don't you know high noon is in the middle of the day, not at 12am?" He just laughed but after punching the galvanizing that day, I knew his temper was ferocious.'

Chapter 18

Muddied Waters

Sliman remembered another job near Brixton Hill but this time with a ferocious footnote. It was an old house that had been broken up into bite-sized living spaces and converted into flats. The waste water wasn't running properly from the building into the sewage system so Sliman and Kelly had to dig out under the property and refix the clasp on the 12-inch pipe that carried the waste water away from the building and off down Brixton Hill.

They broke through the soil down a right of way to the side of the property and pushed scribbled notes through doors, warning residents not to flush water from their toilets while the work was going on. Kelly then dug a narrow tunnel under the house to where the waste pipe coupled with the sewage system. This was the 1970s. Health and safety standards were considerably less rigorous than today and the narrow, vulnerable tunnel felt liable to collapse. As Kelly wiggled into the passage, Sliman imagined having to drag him clear by the ankles.

Out of sight and under the house, Kelly got to work, before an Asian woman living on the third floor of the property forgot about him *and* the note warning residents not to yank the chains of their toilets. Which is exactly what she did and below in the hole Kelly got a jolt. Somewhere up the pipe he could hear the sound of a cistern emptying, then the splashing sound as the water gushed down. Gallons of waste water crashed on top of him.

'I could hear the screams in the hole,' said Sliman. 'He was screaming to get out. It was terrible. He just went mad, and the ground drenched. He went ballistic. I mean he even frightened me.' Kelly wiggled himself free to exit the hole, his hair matted with water and waste, his face covered with dirt and contorted with rage. 'I had to pin him in the hole with the handle of the shovel so he couldn't get out,' said Sliman. 'He started roaring up at the woman in the flat. Calling her every name under the sun.

"Ye fuckin' bitch. Ye Asian bitch. I'll fuckin' kill ye.""

The woman's husband, who was also in the flat, heard the threats and flew into a rage. 'He was a huge man,' said Sliman, 'and he came thundering down the stairs and out into the back of the house. I was actually trying to protect him from Ken, so I pushed him while he was running, but caught him off balance and he ended up going flat on his back in a puddle of water. I was holding Ken in the hole to keep him pinned and he was going crazy. He would have killed the guy if he'd have got him. Actually, he would have gone into the house and killed the woman too, I've no doubt about that.'

I had listened to Sliman cast doubt on Kelly's profile as a cold-blooded killer, but now a counter image was emerging – that of a construction worker who, while popular and charismatic, also possessed a quick, violent temper and a wont for confrontation.

Sliman couldn't identify with Kelly's media persona, his homosexuality, his poor hygiene and that he'd committed the number of murders being reported. Yet, he believed Kelly's rage could bring him to the point of murder. This wasn't speculation – he'd seen it with his own eyes.

He remembered how, after the altercation with the Asian woman and her husband, they still had to finish the job. They returned on a day of rainfall so heavy he had to buy Kelly a pair of Wellingtons boots. But when he came back later that evening he found Kelly missing and the Wellingtons and digging tools laid neatly on the grass beside the hole.

'I'm thinking to myself: "Where could he have gone in his socks?"' He enquired after Kelly in the house where the work was being completed but the woman who answered the door looked just as puzzled. He drove to the nearest cafe, but they hadn't seen anyone matching Kelly's description. It was the same thing in the local pub. But just when he was about to give up, the builder spotted Ken's profile through the window of a neighbour's house next door.

'He was sat at the kitchen table and a woman, an older woman, was cooking him dinner – a big steak dinner and two bottles of Guinness – and Ken had his feet up. He'd got talking to her in the time I was away and not long after, he moved in there.'

The romance moved quickly but was brief. Kelly's rugged charm was not well received by the woman's family. 'She had a grown-up daughter who lived in Reading and she didn't like Ken,' he said. 'She gave some opinion to her mother about him and the mother said it back to Ken and he lost the head, went into a temper.' Gripped by rage, Kelly confronted his lover's daughter.

'I'd a yard down in Brixton then and Cadbury's vans used the yard beside us,' said Sliman. 'Ken went down there to one of the drivers, who was scared of him, and Ken told him to drive him to Reading to where the daughter lived. The guy did and Ken was going mad all the way up there and when he got to the house, he busted his way through a glass door, and started throttling the daughter with the aerial lead off a television set he smashed.

'The woman had called her husband, a taxi driver, and in turn he had called the police. They arrived in a couple of vans to arrest him. But Ken met them on the driveway and they beat him black and blue. Oh they gave Ken a fierce beating.

He was on recall from Broadmoor then and they sent him back I think.

'Once he was sober again, he was fine, like a different person. He was back into work later that week and I could never understand that – how they'd release him so soon. But at the same time he was saying to me: "I gave them hell up there. They knew they were in a fight, I can tell you that much."

'When it went to court, Ken lost the head again. He jumped from the dock and pulled off the judge's cape. The police started flaking [hitting] him, and they hauled him out of the court and managed to get Ken into the back of a small Panda car. They were sitting on top of him in the back but he still managed to kick out two windows of the car. I think he broke one of their arms as well.'

Kelly was eventually subdued outside a court in Reading. Years later, he would be tried and convicted in the Old Bailey for a charge of murder and a charge of manslaughter. But by then, Sliman and Kelly had long parted ways.

Brian Sliman only had cause to think about him again when Kelly's name started popping up in news reports in 2015. That was when he started questioning the claims. 'All these stories that he was dirty, I never saw that,' he said. 'Ken was always clean. When I knew him he always showered and had his hair Brylcreemed back. And when he was sober, you'd never meet a nicer fella. He was never impolite to a client. He'd always start the morning by reading through the paper and he loved Gaelic games.

'But when he had a drink, it would fall forward over his eyes, and it was like he was looking through bars. If Ken had one or two pints, he'd be gone, pissed. But he'd keep going. The rest of the lads would go home.'

And despite the fact that Kelly had been found guilty of murder by a jury, Sliman admitted that he still found it difficult to match a man who could deliver a foot-perfect retake of the Grand National with the murderous monster portrayed in the media. 'To keep it going without a slip, naming horses, and the jumps they were going over. It was an unbelievable skill. People used to call for him to do it and praise him behind his back when he did.

'When all this started coming out about him, my own son said to me: "Do you know what, I'd find it very hard to say anything negative about Ken." He met Ken when he was a kid, and that was the other thing about him – he was brilliant with children. They loved him.'

But even this redeeming quality could be intertwined with Kelly's disposition for causing disorder. 'I remember a group of us leaving the pub this one afternoon,' recalled Sliman. 'It was around lunchtime and Ken was with us. There was a mother with a couple of young kids coming up the street and Ken stooped down and introduced himself. They were asking him questions and he was telling them he was "Uncle Ken". They headed off and one of the guys says to him: "Why were you saying you were Uncle Ken?" And he said: "Sure when the kids go home they'll tell the old man that they met Uncle Ken today and the wife will have some explaining to do to get out of it."'

Uncle Ken. Mad Ken.

'There was no sense to a lot of what he did. But they were the kind of things he would do. Sometimes he'd run into a shop, grab a woman who was buying shoes and say: "Come out of there, they are too expensive," and he'd hurry her out of the shop. He used to get a kick out of doing stuff like that.'

Sliman admitted there was plenty of stuff from Kelly's background he never knew about, and despite them working together for four years, Kelly never mentioned any children or that he'd been married. 'I never knew he had kids,' he said. 'Only that a woman he was with had some children and he had an obvious interest in women. He could be very charming, which makes me convinced he *wasn't* gay.'

That he *was* a gay man struggling to deal with suppressed feelings was at the heart of Platt's portrayal of Kieran Kelly and his motivation to murder. From the *Daily Mail* to the *Daily Express*, the profile of Britain's secret serial killer was that of a homosexual homeless man, who preyed on gay, homeless men. But like the reported murder rates, Sliman struggled with this image, if not Kelly's ferocity. 'He could explode in a moment like a bullet from a gun,' he said. 'If Ken is guilty of what people say he's guilty of, then I'm convinced I saved two people's lives that day in Brixton Hill when the woman flushed the toilet on him.'

Chapter 19

Remains? What Remains?

Sent: 19 September 2016 17:08:38
To: portlaoise_ds@garda.ie
Subject: FAO Eoin Everard

Dear Eoin,

I tried to make contact again today re the Kieran Kelly case (from Rathdowney, convicted of two murders in London in the '80s).

The last time we spoke was in relation to bones found on his former property on the Ballybuggy Road, by Nicky Meagher and then Doctor, Niall O'Doherty, in 1993 and a request made for any information related to this discovery.

My original contact was on July 15. I've since been in contact with the Home Office in London and the British Transport Police and if we can't get an ID or an explanation on the bones then we will have to say that Portlaoise Garda Station failed to provide one after two months and consistent requests.

The find is a feature of the story and we will need to show that we tried, and failed in this case, to get to the bottom of it, through yourselves.

Would you be free to take a call on this?

Best regards

* * *

The meeting with Brian Sliman – and the often conflicting narratives of the Kelly story – had placed a higher demand on the need to accumulate hard evidence. However, post that extraordinary pub conversation, and some weeks after the revelations about skeletal remains discovered on the site of Kelly's home, Gardaí had so far failed to respond to requests for information.

In July 2016, I contacted Gardaí divisional headquarters in Portlaoise, where an officer dealing with the inquiry said follow-ups were being made with retired Gardaí who worked the Rathdowney area in 1993. In the meantime, I'd received a tip-off that named an officer who had worked around Rathdowney during the period the discovery was said to have been made, and had passed on the name of that officer to the Gardaí handler.

After several failed attempts to get answers, it took until 2 August to make contact with the Garda dealing with the information request. He confirmed that he'd spoken to 'an officer' but that he didn't believe him to have been involved in the discovery. And that was all he could say at the time because the retired officer was on holidays.

Then the Garda suggested that the call-out log may not stretch back to 1993 and there may not be anything on the record – never mind any forensic test results – to do with any remains. 'It *is* twenty-three years ago,' reasoned the officer. 'But yeah, you would expect there to be a record of the results.' Two more telephone calls followed but neither led to anything.

But if the enquiries into the discovered remains in Ireland weren't going anywhere, then there had been a significant development in England. Officer A had successfully made contact with one of the original investigators responsible for bringing the Kelly case to the Old Bailey in 1984 – the former detective inspector in Clapham Police Station, Ian Brown. 'He remembers quite a lot about this job, but he doesn't remember Geoff Platt in any shape or form,' he said.

This disclosure by Officer A struck me as unusual considering he had revealed that Platt received a commendation for his work on the case. Officer A also said the original recordings from Kelly's confession had been dug out. These recordings were something Platt claimed to have had a copy of. 'It was transcribed originally in the '80s and used to go to the Attorney General with the authority to charge Kelly, and used with regards to the murder trial,' said Officer A.

'There are murder allegations; a thorough investigation took place and where police could charge they charged,' he added. 'But the number of missing murders – there is no record of those anywhere. Another investigating officer on that case, a detective sergeant, later became the head of homicide command in the Met. I guess if there was a thought he might be able to rekindle some old cases and get charges then I think he probably would have.'

'Listen,' said Officer A. 'I don't want to hang Geoff Platt out to dry here. Like I said before, we are pursuing twenty-four cases linked with Kelly and all we have for certain right now is the Boyd murder and the murder of Hector Fisher in Clapham Common. Maybe this former detective Ian Brown will be able to tell you more.'

Chapter 20

Dancing Man

It was August 1983, in a small box-like interview room in Clapham Police Station. A haze of cigarette smoke lingered around a light hanging from the ceiling and detectives Ian Brown, Ray Adams and Andre Baker took it in turns to question Kieran Kelly. The table was filled with cigarette packets and bluey wisps of smoke floated up towards the light.

Without warning, Kelly jumped from his chair and started to shadow box. A rhythmic flurry of punches exploded from his shoulders. And when he stopped punching, the man began to dance. Ian Brown slumped back in his chair, took a draw on his cigarette, and waited for the performance to finish.

Twenty-four hours earlier he'd arrested the Irishman and charged him with murder after he'd found a homeless tramp, William Boyd, dead in the cells of his police station. The clock had been ticking towards 5pm when Brown heard cries for help echoing down the corridors. He raced to the cells to find his sergeant kneeling on the floor giving the kiss of life to Boyd, a homeless bearded man whose body had already turned cold on the tiles. In the same cell Kieran Kelly was sitting, barefoot, with his legs crossed.

There was a third man in the cell. His name was Paul McManus and he'd been arrested along with Kelly following the robbery of a man called Walter Bell on Clapham Common. It was McManus' terrified screams that sounded about the police station when he'd witnessed Kelly attacking Boyd.

In the cell, Detective Inspector (DI) Brown, could see that a pair of knotted socks had been pulled tight around the victim's neck and he quickly concluded that they belonged to the barefoot man – Kieran Kelly. The bearded man was dead and Brown and his officers hauled Kelly from the cell where he immediately confessed to the murder.

'Boyd was snoring loudly,' said the former DI. 'That was the reason Kelly gave for murdering him. I think he said: "He ain't going to snore no more."'

Kieran Kelly measured up to little more than a bag of bones in DI Brown's estimation. Of average height, wiry, and with a prominent nose, he remembers that first interview and how Kelly fidgeted constantly. 'Everything about him was moving,' said Brown 'And he'd do stupid things. He'd jump from his chair and start shadow boxing. He'd dance. He'd run around the room, hurl abuse and then sit down again.'

Twenty-four hours after the discovery of Boyd, in the interview room of Clapham Police Station, DI Brown doodled on his notebook and waited for his sergeant to bring back more information on Kelly. Within minutes, the latch on the door lifted and his sergeant handed him some hastily scribbled notes he'd retrieved after calling the police archive.

The notes revealed that Kelly had been acquitted on a murder charge six years before Boyd in 1977, and how the victim was another homeless man, Edward Toal. Brown sensed he might be on to something. He had a man sitting in front of him who had just confessed to the murder of a homeless vagrant, and had previously been acquitted of the murder of another homeless man. But he didn't know then that he was about to pull the thread on a confession of mass murder. And he never expected that thirty odd years later, long after he'd retired, the case would be making news headlines again.

'Can you stop the tape for a moment please?' asked Brown, leaning across the dining room table of a golf club just outside the town of Sevenoaks in Kent. It was a hot September morning and he was sitting to the rear of the room, by the door into the kitchen that screeched every time the staff went in to collect service. This meeting had only come about on the say so of Officer A. And Brown, who had led the investigation on the Kelly case, only agreed to meet on the condition that he felt comfortable.

He'd never gone on the record about Kelly. He'd never felt like he needed to, until the story started making headlines and he ended up talking to police investigators about his own role in the original investigation.

Through the open door of the restaurant it was possible to hear the sound of golf balls pinging in the distance. 'I've never spoken about the Kelly case publicly,' said Brown. 'Bar giving talks on cruise ships. This only all came back up again last year when Geoff Platt started saying it was a cover-up.'

He unzipped his laptop bag, fished a couple of A4 sheets from a plastic cover and placed his CV on the table. It listed cases involving the notorious London crime family, the Krays, the investigation into the Brink's-Mat gold bullion robbery, and later, a secondment to the Caribbean where Brown had been sent to help break an international drugs ring. It also said *he* was the detective who built the case that sent Kelly to prison. That was more than thirty years ago, long before Platt's claims and a commitment from Sir Bernard Hogan-Howe to look into the case.

In contrast with Platt, Brown was a cautious and somewhat reluctant contributor. This meeting, like the re-emergence of the Kelly story, felt like an unwelcome inconvenience on his retirement. But it was probably necessary to help put the record straight. For him, the real starting point to the disputed story of serial murder was when he learned in the interview room in

Clapham that Kelly was acquitted of murdering Edward Toal in Kennington Park in 1977.

From his seat in the corner of the golf club, Brown raised his arm to catch the attention of the waitress. 'Two coffees please, blossom,' he smiled. 'Right,' he said, looking at the recorder on the table. 'You can turn it on again now.'

Chapter 21

The Tombstone

It was a feature of the Kelly story that the killer's alleged crimes didn't reveal themselves in chronological order. The investigation was anchored by the two convictions for manslaughter of William Boyd and the killing of Hector Fisher, but revelations about other alleged murder confessions jumped between the timeline, running from claims of Christy Smith in 1953 to Boyd, the final murder, thirty years later in 1983. According to the original investigator, this was the order in which Kelly confessed to the murders he committed.

After he'd confessed to Boyd, the next case linked with Kelly was the one, the only one, that appeared on his police record – a case of murder acquittal involving a man called Edward Toal in Kennington Park, that Brown and investigators discovered on the defendant's case file from 1977.

The landscape of Kennington hadn't changed that much since Brown was a serving officer. In the tube station, a winding staircase spiralled the seventy-nine steps to the surface. And on this weekday morning, a drip-drip of commuters emerged with purposeful haste from the exit and took off in different directions down Kennington Park Road, which ran like a black river of tarmac transporting red buses and cyclists into central London.

The walk down towards Oval cricket ground was a pathway paved with worn flagstones and lined with mature leafy trees whose trunks were blackened from decades spent soaking up innumerable tons of nitrogen dioxide emitted by exhaust fumes. Old Georgian buildings with tall, single-glazed windows stood back from the passing traffic, with brickwork similarly discoloured by the dirty air that crop-dusted the street.

From this urban setting, Kennington Park emerged like an unruly patch of green, in the borough of Lambeth. A sign by the entrance revealed that the park opened in 1854 and it had a long history of idleness in a city that limited peaceful moments. On this late summer morning in 2016, dog walkers stood about in the park talking, and behind them the city's skyline loomed above the leafy reaches of mature trees.

But the park had a dark history. In the past, when the evening sun stooped low behind these trees, homeless men and women who had spent the day begging change, riding tube lines to stay warm or looking for a public toilet to grab a wash, started filtering through the gates to hide out, get wasted and find somewhere to sleep. Many were dodging London's strict vagrancy rules, which would have left them locked up if they were caught begging or sleeping rough on the street. One of the homeless people who used to use the park was Edward Toal.

In 1977 there was a cemetery in the park and scattered among the headstones were flat tombstones upon which homeless people often slept. The dancing man, Kieran Kelly, was also known to have slept in the park. And in the spring of 1977, Kelly returned to Kennington Park to discover Edward Toal passed out on the tombstone where he wanted to sleep. This simple decision of where to lie down was the pretext to murder, according to two other rough sleepers who, explained Brown, watched Kelly emerge from the darkness and stop by the sleeping Toal.

Brown said they watched as Kelly slowly removed a length of rope tied around his waist, which he'd been using to hold up his trousers, and ran it through his hands. With the sound of car engines breezing into central London behind the tree line, Kelly twisted the ends of the rope around the palm of each of his hands and, leaning down, looped the noose around Toal's head. Then, bracing himself, he pulled his hands tight into a clench so they met behind the sleeping man's neck.

Toal kicked out and wriggled but after a few seconds Kelly released his grip and relieved the tension. Toal's body fell limp but he was still breathing when Kelly untangled his hands from the rope and walked away. Brown recalled that one of two men, who would later become witnesses, shouted through the darkness: 'You almost killed him there, Kelly.'

It was an observation that stopped Kelly in his tracks and he turned and walked back to the tombstone where Toal was lying. He rewrapped the ends of the rope around his hands again and for the second time, looped the noose round the man's head. He pulled again, harder this time, and Toal scrambled with his feet to try and find some kind of grip on the headstone in an effort to wriggle free. He was fighting to fill his lungs with air but Kelly doubled down on his squeeze until the life force left Toal.

When his body fell limp, Kelly stood back, untangled his hands from the rope and retied it around the waist of his trousers. 'Then he turned around to the watching men and said: "I have now,"' explained Brown.

The former detective inspector recounted that Kelly was soon picked up, arrested and remanded in custody for the murder of Toal and that his case was heard in the Old Bailey. 'But of course it took a number of months for the case to go to trial,' he declared, sipping coffee.

Kelly was sent to prison where he awaited trial but after a few months, the blood coursing through his veins had started to run alcohol free. The defendant was sober, rested, nourished and free from the anxiety that weighed so heavily on his shoulders out on the common. He was a man transformed.

Brown didn't know all this when his sergeant gave him the scribbled note. It wasn't until later that he discovered the case relied heavily on the testimony of the two witnesses who'd told officers they'd watched on as Kelly garroted the stricken Toal with a length of rope he'd pulled from his trousers.

But while Kelly rested and awaited the start of his trial, the star witnesses remained snared by addiction and vagrancy. When they arrived at the Old Bailey, the men cut a dishevelled, shambling sight especially when measured against a now sober and suited Kelly. And when the men took the stand, they contradicted each other's evidence, and proved to be poor witnesses to their own story. They were earnest, but their physical and mental condition made it extremely difficult for them to give a reliable account of what had happened to Edward Toal in Kennington Park that spring night.

'By the time the trial comes around, Kelly's been inside for a couple of months,' declared Brown. 'He's smart and off the wine and spirits. He looks normal, and pleads his innocence. The only real evidence against him is from two meths drinkers, who by the way, are still drinking meths, and are still living rough. And their evidence isn't deemed credible so Kelly walks on an acquittal.'

In the police station interview room in Clapham in 1983, Brown said he didn't have access to that level of detail on the case. But after the murder of Boyd in the cell, his gut told him the prosecution had failed to close the case. 'I thought to myself: "We've got him for William Boyd. He's admitted that. Maybe *now*, he'll admit to Toal."'

Only Kelly didn't. Even though the former DI was absolutely certain the judge had got it wrong and Kelly was responsible. Brown didn't know it at the time, but sitting in that box-like interview room in Clapham Police Station in 1983, he was about to ask one of *the* most important questions of his career. A question that elicited a response from Kelly that no one in the room saw coming; a response that started with a murder admission, two years before the Toal case, that went all the way back to 1953, and returned right back to present day.

'I said: "Right then Kelly, tell me about all the other murders," thinking he might confess to Toal, the one he'd been acquitted for in Kennington in '77.

'But then Kelly replied: "Which one are you talking about?"

"You just tell me," I said.

'And he said: "You're talking about Fisher aren't you?"

'"Yep, that's the one," I replied not having a clue who Fisher was. And then – after Boyd and Toal, I started nodding at my station sergeant to call the archives and find out who the hell Fisher was.'

The sergeant hurried away to contact the police archive and the investigation team waited for him to return with anything they could find related to someone called Fisher. 'And it turns out the case he's talking about is another case again, from two years earlier than Toal, in 1975,' said Brown. 'A guy called Hector Fisher was beaten and stabbed to death at Clapham Common and that was unsolved. No one was ever picked up for the murder and here's Kelly sitting in the interview room in Clapham Police Station, eight years later, telling us he's done it.'

CERTIFIED COPY OF AN ENTRY
Pursuant to the Births and Deaths Registration Act 1953

BBL 725515

DEATH	Entry No. 199

Registration district Durham Central

Administrative area County of Durham

Sub-district Durham

1. **Date and place of death**
Sixth April 2001
55 Finchale Avenue Brasside Durham

2. **Name and surname**
Kieran Patrick KELLY

3. **Sex** Male

4. **Maiden surname of woman who has married**

5. **Date and place of birth**
17th March 1930   Dublin

6. **Occupation and usual address**
----
55 Finchale Avenue Brasside Durham

7. (a) **Name and surname of informant**
Certificate received from A. Tweddle Coroner for North District of Durham. Inquest held the 16th day of October 2001

(b) **Qualification**

(c) **Usual address**

8. **Cause of death**
I (a) Chronic Obstructive Airways Disease

Verdict Natural Causes

9. I certify that the particulars given by me above are true to the best of my knowledge and belief

Signature of informant

10. **Date of registration**
Eighteenth October 2001

11. **Signature of registrar**
M. Corner Registrar

Certified to be a true copy of an entry in a register in my custody.

Deputy *Superintendent Registrar *Registrar—

*Strike out whichever does not apply

Date 7·10·2016

CAUTION: THERE ARE OFFENCES RELATING TO FALSIFYING OR ALTERING A CERTIFICATE AND USING OR POSSESSING A FALSE CERTIFICATE. ©CROWN COPYRIGHT
WARNING: A CERT...

A copy of Kieran Kelly's death certificate. See location of death under section one and usual address under section 6, which challenges the view the convicted killer died in prison.

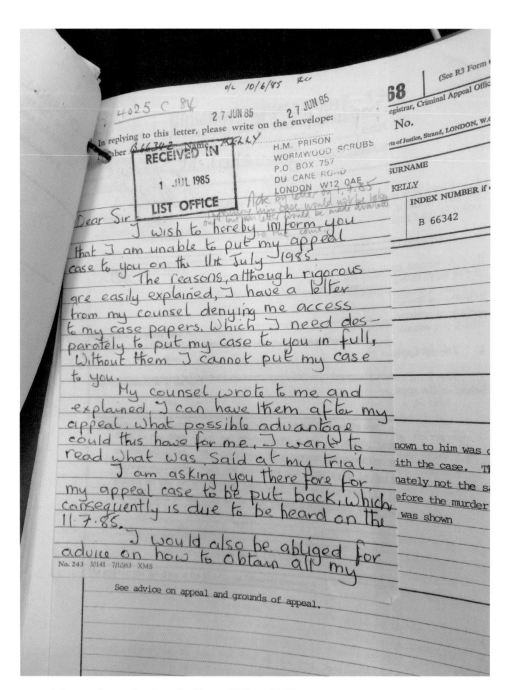

In replying to this letter, please write on the envelope:
number ___ Name: KELLY

H.M. PRISON
WORMWOOD SCRUBS
P.O BOX 757
DU CANE ROAD
LONDON W12 0AE

68   (See R3 Form

egistrar, Criminal Appeal Offic

No.

rts of Justice, Strand, LONDON, W.

SURNAME

KELLY

INDEX NUMBER if

B 66342

Dear Sir,
     I wish to hereby inform you
that I am unable to put my appeal
case to you on th 11th July 1985.
     The reasons, although rigorous
are easily explained, I have a letter
from my counsel denying me access
to my case papers, Which I need des-
parately to put my case to you in full.
Without them I cannot put my case
to you.
     My counsel wrote to me and
explained, I can have them after my
appeal. What possible advantage
could this have for me, I want to
read what was said at my trial.
     I am asking you therefore for
my appeal case to be put back, which
consequently is due to be heard on the
11 7.85.
     I would also be abliged for
advice on how to obtain all my

nown to him was
ith the case. T
nately not the s
efore the murder
was shown

No. 243 30141 7/10/63 XMS

See advice on appeal and grounds of appeal.

A letter of appeal written by Kieran Kelly in 1985.

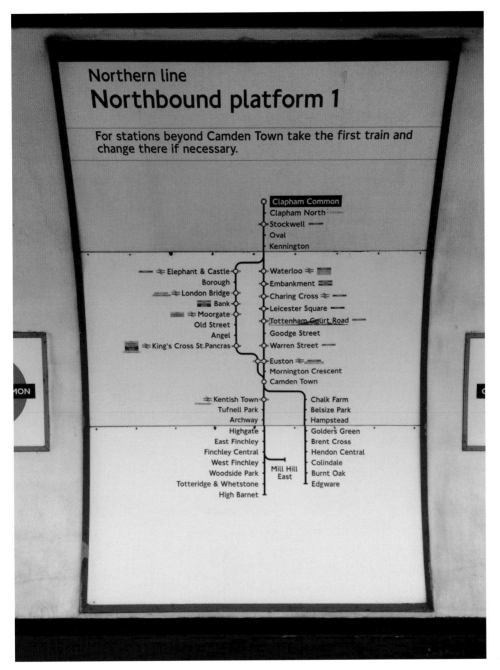

A map of the Northern Line of The London Underground. Kieran Kelly confessed to multiple crimes on the network.

To the Registrar, Criminal Appeal

REF. No.

Royal Courts of Justice, Strand, London, W.C.2

TO BE FILED.

COURT OF APPEAL
CRIMINAL DIVISION

FORM
O

REQUEST TO
THE REGISTRAR

SURNAME

KELLY

Particulars
of
APPELLANT

FULL NAMES
Block letters

FORENAMES

KIERAN PATRICK KELLY.

ADDRESS
If detained give address where
detained and if detained in
prison give prison number.

H.M.P. WORMSCRUBS PRISON
No B 66342.

PART 1
SEE NOTES ON BACK

Set out the request under the appropriate heading.
A separate form must be used for each request.

I do not wish to Be at Court for
my application for leave to appeal and
extension of time.
My Council will present my
case in full to the Court. I do hope you
understand this Request.

Thanking all

(Signed)

(Appellant)

Date
9/7/85.

For Use in Criminal Appeal Office
Received

RECEIVED IN

12 JUL 1985

LIST OFFICE

PART 2
FOR USE IN THE CRIMINAL APPEAL OFFICE

A Request to The Registrar, written by Kieran Kelly in 1985.

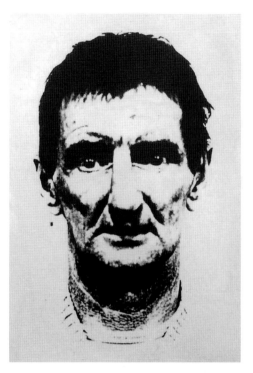

A portrait of Kieran Kelly aged in his 50s.

A typical evening scene outside Clapham Common Underground Station in London. Kieran Kelly was convicted of murdering Hector Fisher just yards from this location.

Clapham Common at night where Kieran Kelly socialized and later, murdered, Hector Fisher.

Clapham Common Underground Station with its distinctive island platform. Ex-policeman Geoff Platt claimed Kieran Kelly exploited this setting to commit murder.

Former policeman Geoff Platt who brought the Kieran Kelly story back into the public arena in 2015.

Holy Trinity church in Clapham Common, close to where Hector Fisher was murdered in 1975.

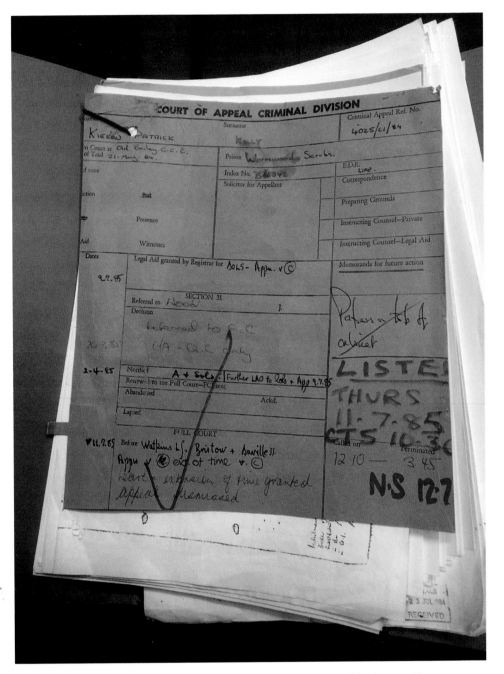

Just some of Kieran Kelly's court files sourced in The National Archives in Kew.

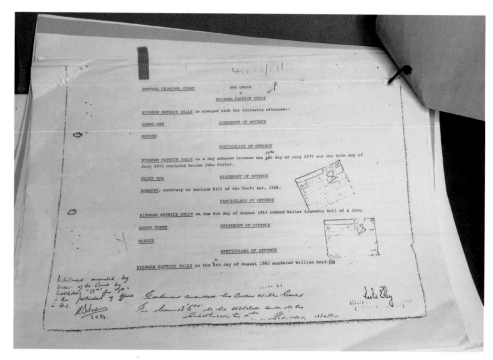

Kieran Kelly's charge sheet from the Central Criminal Court.

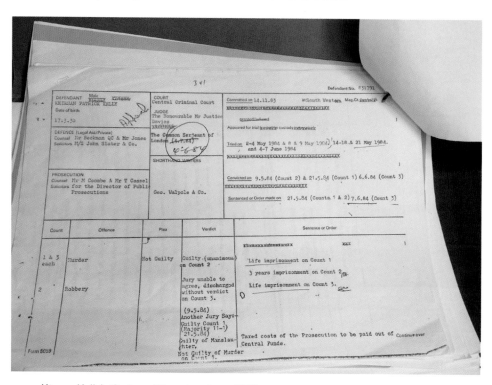

Kieran Kelly's Order of Sentence from 1985.

A former home of Kieran Kelly on Waldegrave Road in Crystal Palace, London

Michael Creagh, local historian in Rathdowney in County Laois.

Nicky Meagher, close to where he discovered remains, at his home on the Ballybuggy Road in Rathdowney, County Laois.

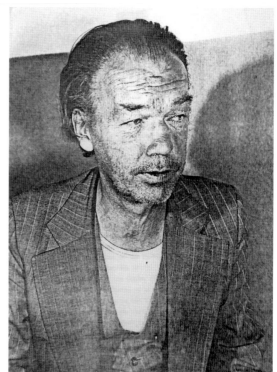

Paul McManus, who witnessed the murder of William Boyd in the cells of Clapham Police Station in 1984.

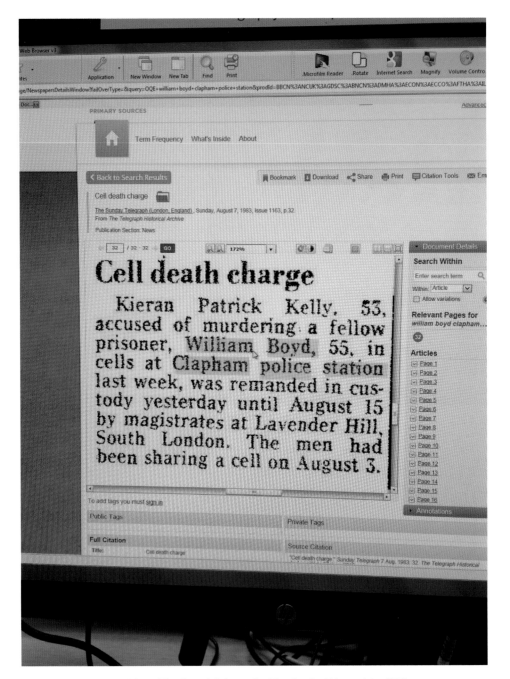

Doc...

Advanced

PRIMARY SOURCES

Term Frequency   What's Inside   About

< Back to Search Results   Bookmark   Download   Share   Print   Citation Tools   Em

Cell death charge

The Sunday Telegraph (London, England) , Sunday, August 7, 1983, Issue 1163, p.32
From *The Telegraph Historical Archive*

Publication Section: News

32 / 32 - 32   GO   172%

Document Details

Search Within

Enter search term

Within: Article

Allow variations

Relevant Pages for
william boyd clapham...

Articles
Page 1
Page 2
Page 3
Page 4
Page 5
Page 6
Page 7
Page 8
Page 9
Page 10
Page 11
Page 12
Page 13
Page 14
Page 15
Page 16

Cell death charge

Kieran Patrick Kelly, 53, accused of murdering a fellow prisoner, William Boyd, 55, in cells at Clapham police station last week, was remanded in custody yesterday until August 15 by magistrates at Lavender Hill, South London. The men had been sharing a cell on August 3.

To add tags you must sign in

Annotations

Public Tags

Private Tags

Full Citation
Title: Cell death charge

Source Citation
"Cell death charge." *Sunday Telegraph* 7 Aug. 1983: 32. *The Telegraph Historical*

Report sourced from The British Library by *The Sunday Telegraph* in 1983.

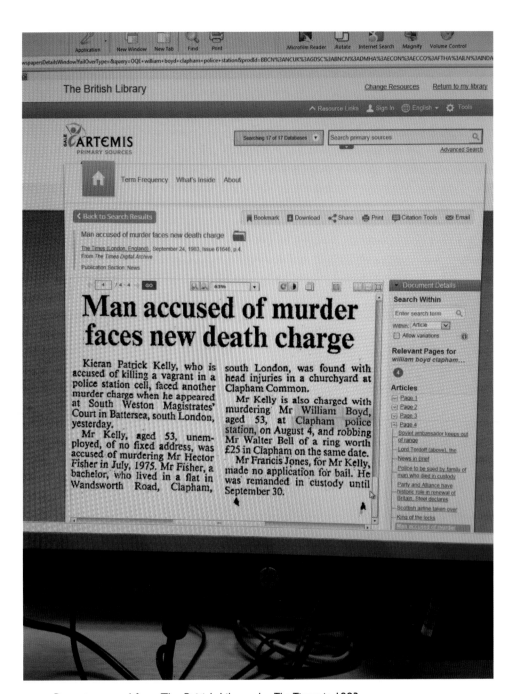

Report sourced from The British Library by *The Times in* 1983.

The main square in Kieran Kelly's hometown of Rathdowney in County Laois, Ireland.

Chapter 22

Fisher

Thanks to Ian Brown, the Kelly case had a substantive counterpoint to the loose testimony of the former policeman Platt. Here was an investigator from the original team willing to disclose what Kelly had apparently claimed to have done, in addition to the two murders he'd been convicted of. Victims, motives, crime scenes – Brown could reflect with some authority on the killer's case file. There were still more questions than answers such as what happened at Clapham Common tube station, discounted by Officer A as a murder scene but still at the centre of Kelly's billing in the media as the London Underground serial killer.

Before meeting Brown in Kent, and after meeting with Platt in Stoke, I visited the station at Clapham Common. According to Platt's story and the now-popular media narrative, it was at stations such as Clapham Common that Kelly hurled victims on to the tracks. It was claimed he utilized the station's barrier-free island platform to attack vulnerable commuters, using stealth and the cover of other passengers to attack and then blend into the crowd. Only there was no record of any deaths linked with Kelly from this tube station or any other.

The other murder that had seeped into the public consciousness in London *and* Rathdowney didn't happen on the underground but above ground on the common itself.

97

Back in the interview room in 1983, after Kelly had confessed to the murder of William Boyd, Brown had expected the Irishman to confess to the murder he was acquitted of in the Old Bailey in 1977 – Edward Toal. But instead, when the detective inspector asked him about 'all the other murders', Kelly caught him cold by throwing out a name he'd never heard before – Hector Fisher – who they quickly discovered was a one-time successful businessman who'd been found dead on Clapham Common.

Brown's station sergeant had returned to the smoky interview room with case notes from the police archive that gave them a fix on the murder location. 'It told me this guy, Fisher, had been murdered at the back of the common,' said Brown, still seated in the golf club dining room. 'And after murdering Boyd in the cells, and reading the details of the Edward Toal case, we have Kelly telling us about this one, which was never solved and we started to question him about that.'

The former DI explained that in 1975, detectives had discovered a body at the back of Holy Trinity church on Clapham Common, which had suffered multiple stab wounds and blunt force trauma injuries. Detectives found two £20 notes in one of the pockets and later discovered that this sum of money would prove significant in linking Kelly to the crime. Brown also learned that police had interviewed scores of suspects over the Fisher murder, including Kelly. And that the case, then eight years old, had been gathering dust on the shelf marked 'Unsolved' in the vaults of Scotland Yard.

The record showed that Hector Fisher's body had been found slumped on a bench close to the church and just a couple of hundred yards from the tube station. It was a murder that registered because rumours circulated that the body had been attacked with a broken bottle that had also been used to mutilate Fisher's genitals. Witnesses remembered how some nights before he died, Fisher had been spotted visiting an off-licence in Clapham with another man known to be a drinker on the common. They remembered because the two had made an unlikely pair – Fisher, the once-prosperous businessman, and the rugged street drinker.

Using archive case notes and Kelly's rambling testimony, Brown and his team started piecing together the Fisher murder with Kelly, the self-confessed leading man. In one particular statement made to police in 1983, Kelly told Brown and fellow officers that it was him that 'cut' Fisher. That they'd met in the park earlier that day and that he'd followed him to the church that night.

'Why did you kill him?' asked Brown.

'Because he was a dirty old cunt,' replied Kelly. 'I gave him a wallop, stabbed him, and took some money, but I left some money on him.'

'Why did you do that?' queried the detective inspector.

'To fuck the cops,' replied Kelly. 'So you wouldn't think it was a robbery.'

'So it wasn't a robbery, Kelly?' Brown wondered.

'No, he was a dirty old bastard,' said Kelly. 'He used to dress up in women's clothes. He was a fucking puff.'

'What about the knife?' asked Brown. 'Where did you throw it?'

'I threw it in the council yard,' said Kelly. 'They put all the rubbish there, ye know. I was far too clever for you.'

'And how do you figure that then Kelly?' asked Brown.

'The police didn't realize it *was* a robbery,' he replied. 'I covered it up.'

'And how did you do that?' asked the DI, massaging Kelly's ego.

'I left £40 in the pocket of Hector Fisher's coat. Two £20 notes.'

The amount of money left on the body was something only the murderer could have known, explained Brown, recalling the to-and-fro of the exchange in the interview room. And in a sense the disclosure of that action resonated with Platt's story of how the young Kelly purportedly stashed porn but in a way that it would be found by his mother.

'After the beating, Kelly rummaged through his pockets, took some money but made sure to leave money on him so as to confuse the police,' added Brown. 'I asked him why did he do it and he said: "Well, he wanted my arse so I stabbed him and I stabbed him in the bollocks." So now we have Kelly admitting to the Fisher murder but strangely not one he was acquitted for – Edward Toal. Then I said to him: "Tell me then, Kelly, when did all this start?" and he said: "It all started in 1953 with the murder of a friend of mine – Christy Smith."'

Chapter 23

Killing Spree

Along with the killings of Boyd and Fisher, and even the acquittal of Edward Toal, the name Christy Smith had become one of the touchstones of the Kelly story. But unlike Boyd, Fisher and Toal, the Smith case had failed to make it to court.

Ian Brown stretched his legs out from the table in the golf club, took a deep breath and signalled for the waitress. 'Two more coffees please, blossom,' he nodded. Through an open door, beside which an air-conditioning unit hummed in a high gear, golfers started to file from the sunshine into the shade of the clubhouse. Bursts of laughter and the sound of glasses clinking could be heard down the far end of the room.

The former detective inspector had been talking about the Kelly case for less than an hour. Unlike Platt's testimony, Brown's recall had so far been digestible and orderly. And his memory of those parts of the Kelly confession that had been kept from the public, and out of court, remained clear.

During those early hours in the interview room in Clapham, he told how Kelly had given him the starting point in a chaotic timeline of murder confessions. 'After I'd asked Kelly when did it all start, Kelly said: "In 1953, when I come over with a friend of mine for the Queen's coronation. We was down the tube, I'd had a drink, got cross and threw him under a train in Baker Street Station." And then Kelly started to ramble,' recalled Brown. 'It was as much as we could do to keep up.'

Brown said that Kelly was in the mood for talking that day and he and his fellow officers listened in astonishment to a confession of murders that ran into double figures. The Boyd killing was just the release pin on a story that spiralled into a history of murder claims. The notetaker had to scribble furiously just to keep up. Brown had only become aware of the existence of Kieran Kelly the previous afternoon. But listening to the confession in the interview room in Clapham Police Station, he started to wonder if he'd hit upon the biggest case of his career.

Years later, sitting in the golf club in Kent, he laid out the chronology of Kelly's admissions of murder and attempted murder. But, just as the debunked detective Platt had suggested, there was a long gap – twenty years – between Kelly's first murder admission from 1953 and his second alleged victim, Scotch Jack, who he claimed to have beaten to death with an iron bar in Vauxhall in 1973. Kelly quickly confessed to two more murders that year – one in Bournemouth where he said he stabbed a man to death, and the other, a homeless man in Shepherd's Bush whom he said he kicked to death.

Kelly had already confessed to how and why he'd murdered Hector Fisher on Clapham Common in 1975. And in 1976, he said he'd visited a flat in Coronation Buildings, Vauxhall, which was a well-known drinking spot. There was a man there who Kelly didn't know, but he force-fed him alcohol. The man suffocated to death on his own vomit.

The following year, 1977, Kelly was acquitted for the murder of Edward Toal in Kennington Park. And there was another acquittal in 1982, when he'd been charged with attempted murder at Tooting Bec tube station. The victim this time was the same Francis Taylor that had been namechecked by the security source, Officer A, but misidentified by Platt. Kelly said – and it was quickly confirmed – that he'd thrown Taylor on to the tracks at Tooting Bec Station but the victim had survived, and later, decided against pressing charges because he and Kelly were friends.

That same year, 1977, Kelly confessed to the murder of a man called Mickey Dunne whom he described as homeless and an alcoholic. They'd gone drinking together near the library in Tooting Broadway before Kelly fixed Dunne a deadly cocktail of surgical spirit mixed with orange juice and loaded the drink with prescription drugs. He watched the unsuspecting Dunne drink the deadly potion then gave him a terrible beating when he was incapacitated. Dunne died in King's College Hospital a short time later, and Brown claimed the murder went unnoticed because the cause of death was given as cirrhosis of the liver. The doctors just assumed they were dealing with a man who'd overdosed on alcohol and prescription drugs.

The former DI claimed that Kelly confessed to poisoning another homeless man to death around the same time, using a cocktail of white spirit, and also to setting fire to a building being used as a shelter by street drinkers and addicts. Brown wasn't certain of the details on either of those cases, only that the man who drank the white spirit died in hospital and that other homeless alcoholics had positively identified Kelly as the arsonist who burned down the building.

In 1983, it was claimed that Kelly attacked another homeless man, Jock Gordon, at Oval Underground Station. And in what sounded like a carbon copy of the Taylor case, Kelly ended up flinging the man in front of a train after an altercation on the platform. He, too, miraculously survived. However, William Boyd wasn't so lucky after he found himself locked up with Kelly in Clapham Police Station in August of '83.

Iron bars.

Knives.

Boots.

Lengths of rope.

Poisoning.

Knotted socks.

Kelly's means of murder were many but those who suffered at his hands all shared the same profile. Kelly had a 'type', a typical victim, and there was a pattern to his killing. Because with the exception of Hector Fisher, all of Kelly's victims were homeless and male. They were people who lived bleary lives in the half-light of London's parks and commons; they were people on the margins of society, lost to addiction and struggling with mental health issues.

For Brown, Kelly's confession of murder was chilling for its callous targeting of the vulnerable and the creative ways he'd claimed to have gone about his killing. Brown said he and his fellow investigators tried to make sense of his confession by laying out his admissions in date order.

- 1953, Baker Street, a man named as Christy Smith, pushed on to the tracks
- 1973, Vauxhall, Scotch Jack hit over the head with a bar and buried opposite the Tate Library
- 1973, Bournemouth, unknown male stabbed with a knife
- 1973, Shepherd's Bush, unknown male kicked to death
- 1975, Clapham Common, Hector Fisher, beaten and stabbed to death
- 1976, Coronation Buildings, man force-fed alcohol until he choked on his vomit
- 1977, Kennington Park, Edward Toal, strangled to death (acquitted)
- 1982, Tooting Bec, attempted murder of Francis Taylor, (acquitted)
- 1982, Tooting, the poisoning of Mickey Dunne
- Circa 1982, Peckham Rye poisoning, arson attack on building
- 1983, Oval tube station, attempted murder of Jock Gordon (case dropped)

- 1983, Clapham Police Station, strangulation of William Boyd

'Kelly was confessing to all these murders,' said Brown. 'But generally speaking, if a tramp is found dead, it comes out in the autopsy that they'd suffered a bang to the head and people come to the conclusion that they'd fallen over stone drunk. And with the exception of Smith – who we were unable to trace by the way – the thing about his confession was they were all homeless tramps.'

Chapter 24

The Prince and the Pauper

It was a warm August morning in 1983. The window of the car solicitor John Slater was travelling in was down and he had half an ear on the BBC's morning news bulletin. Then a headline caught his attention: 'A man has been found dead in the cells of Clapham Common Police Station,' said the female newsreader. Slater turned to his business associate driving the car and said: 'I wonder whether Kieran is responsible for it.'

The two solicitors fell back into conversation and forgot about the news, until later in the day when the phone in their office rang. It was Clapham Police Station. There'd been a murder in the cells, and they were calling on behalf of a Kieran Kelly.

* * *

Nearly thirty-four years on from that telephone call, September's sun set a burn across the late evening sky in south-west London. And outside the window of his second-floor practice on the Upper Richmond Road in Putney, shafts of light cut through the alleyways of buildings on Putney High Street and into John Slater's office. Through an open window it was possible to hear the weary CLACK-CLACK of trains pulling in and out of East Putney Underground Station nearby. About the room, thick folders had been stacked in half-orderly piles and down one end, an old clock counted time. At the other end of the room, Slater sat behind his desk.

Using archive news reports from the British Library, I'd been trying to make contact with Kelly's defence team for months. But the QC, Michael Beckman, whose name was listed in *The Daily Telegraph* and *The Times*, was dead and I was unable to make any contact with a Francis Jones. However, to my surprise, I learned that John Slater was still practising. I made an appointment to speak to him about the Kelly case.

'This isn't totally out of the blue,' said Slater from behind his desk. 'The police have already contacted me about claims made by Geoff Platt. So, let's just see what you want to ask me. But I must explain, I don't have any file papers. Some years after the case, instructing solicitors said to send the whole file to them in Wakefield. I was happy to do that because it saved me storage space, so all this will be from memory.'

After a long afternoon spent interviewing Brown, and numerous follow-up phone calls, the Kelly story had unearthed another historical witness. Yet just like the former DI, John Slater could call upon no files that would help him to tell the Kelly story. He, too, would have to rely upon his power of recall.

'It was professional, our relationship and I didn't dislike him,' said Slater. 'It was obvious he was up to no good but often it's easier to deal with hardened criminals who do not expect to go anywhere but prison, and more difficult to deal with people who are first-time offenders.'

'How many cases did you represent him in?' I asked.

'Well, I first represented him over an alleged push under the tube at Tooting Bec Station.'

Tooting Bec was where Francis Taylor had been pushed on to the line in 1982, and in the weeks that followed that attack Slater remembered being handed a file to read in a quiet room in a London court. This in itself wasn't unusual – Slater had more than ten years' experience by that point of his career. Often, he got handed defence cases by the state. Only this wasn't a typical case. His client was a 51-year-old Irishman on trial for the attempted murder of a man called Francis Taylor at Tooting Bec Station on the Northern Line of the London Underground. According to the adjoining notes he'd read in the case file, Kelly was accused of hurling Taylor in front of a train.

Slater understood that Kelly and Taylor were down-and-outs who had possibly been drawn to the Clapham area and south-west London postcodes because of the charitable food services that sometimes pitched up there. Taylor wasn't a serious criminal, just the kind that could tangle up Britain's criminal justice system with a litany of minor offences. He knew that in Taylor and Kelly's world, paranoia and violence set the tempo. The rules that helped to maintain civility in society didn't hold when night enveloped London's commons.

However, an attack that led to someone being pushed on to the rail tracks *was* unusual. Slater understood that Taylor survived because he'd fallen into a service well running just below the tracks. Somewhat remarkably, the train had backed up and the man had walked away. But later, the police picked Kelly up and charged him with attempted murder.

Notable as this incident was, he didn't imagine he was about to acquire the most remarkable client of his career. That first afternoon, he'd heard a rap on the door and had flicked the file closed. Then the handle turned to reveal his client – lean, middle-aged and greying. In that moment it occurred to Slater that he was alone with someone who'd been charged with attempted murder.

He invited Kelly to sit down. They talked and his new client seemed agreeable, charming even, and just like the experience of the builder Brian Sliman, Kelly's pleasant demeanour was at odds with the violent criminal Slater had just been reading about minutes before in the case notes. 'I got on with him perfectly well,' he said, raising the tone of his voice a couple of octaves to denote his own surprise.

And now, in his office in Putney, he was determined to put it on the record that the presentation of Kelly in the press as an unintelligent, low-skilled worker was at odds with his own estimation, which closely mirrored the view of Brian Sliman. 'You could have a conversation with him,' said Slater. 'He understood concepts. You could discuss things with him. He wasn't difficult to deal with and I didn't find him as unintelligent as the IQ results implied. I didn't dislike him. I mean, he wasn't someone who I'd have considered socializing with. And it might have helped that I went on to supply him with kebabs and cigarettes, but then, you had to do that in those days, and I would have done that for all my criminal clients.'

During these meetings, and ones that followed later, the image of his client continued to broaden as Kelly assumed layers of personality beyond his simple billing as a violent criminal. In the fight for the truth in the Kelly story, this challenged the profile presented by both Brown and Platt, and chimed in parts with the one portrayed by Sliman. 'I remember I had to get him a radio one time,' said Slater. 'He wanted to listen to Liverpool for some match – he was a fan I think.

'He did keep the company of down-and-outs and during the course of the trial it came out that the reason Clapham Common was a hang out was because a vicar had set up a soup kitchen there and word got around that there was free food. But then Kieran had jobs from time to time. He was not always hanging about on benches. He'd do some painting and top up his dole money. And it was also my sense that he didn't get as drunk as some of the others did.

'Like I said, I first represented him on Tooting Bec. He was acquitted of that offence in 1982 and then I represented him on a matter of murder at Clapham Police Station and he was charged with the murder of Fisher on Clapham Common. There were those two cases and the one with Francis Taylor on the tube at Tooting Bec.

'He never admitted any of them to me. Very frequently you find what clients say to lawyers and non-lawyers is very different. He would have known that had he admitted anything to a lawyer then they would have been bound by that and he would have known not to do it. I have had cases where I represented clients and they have admitted their offence to third parties, but not to me.

'A double murder case was a big case for me, the most serious case I had to deal with up to then, *and* since. It was an unusual case. Cases like this come along once in your career. I never had a multiple murder case, ever! This is the only one I had.

'But I'd no qualms dealing with him and never felt threatened by him. If you met him here you would think he was a normal bloke and you'd have a conversation with him. You would never think he was capable of some of these crimes more than anyone else. And I never got the impulse off him that he was violent. You do get people you feel threatened by, but I never did with him.' Slater paused for a moment and looked at the clock. 'Sorry,' he said. 'Do you know how long we are going to be?'

Only half an hour had passed since I arrived, and the sun had sunk further behind the buildings on Putney High Street, but inside his upstairs office Kelly's former solicitor had cast new light on the crime story of his former client. It was an image that fit more neatly beside that presented by the builder, Sliman. And significantly, a credible secondary source was casting doubt on Kelly's culpability as a mass murderer. There was also a tangible feeling in the upstairs office that the solicitor had an allegiance to his former client that was rooted in their personal, as well as their professional, relationship.

'Do you feel now that he was capable of some of these crimes that have been attributed to him?' I asked.

'I think he was capable,' he reasoned. 'But I have grave doubts he did them.'

'Grave doubts, really?' I asked.

'It was *never* proven that Kelly killed anyone on the underground first of all,' continued Slater. 'And I felt Kelly was a fantasist. Bear in mind, this was an era when there was more than one multiple murderer.'

He made reference to Peter Sutcliffe, the English serial killer dubbed the Yorkshire Ripper who, in 1981, was convicted of murdering thirteen women; and Dennis Nilsen, who was jailed for life in 1983 after admitting killing fifteen young men, mainly homosexuals, at his home in Muswell Hill, north London. 'I did have cause to wonder if Kelly just wanted the infamy of being a mass murderer,' added Slater.

Chapter 25

Taking Stock

The investigation into the life and crimes of Kieran Kelly had become a story of limits set at opposing ends by the former policeman Geoff Platt and the solicitor John Slater. The story felt like it was being wrenched back and forth between the extremities of these two fixed positions – two murders and thirty-one murders. Brown's story of a confession that totalled more than a dozen murder admissions held the centre ground. Then there was the body in Ireland, and Brian Sliman's alternative profile of Kelly as a personable but volatile man to consider.

Before meeting with Slater, I'd called Officer A to test Platt's claims that members of the public had come forward over deaths on the Northern Line; deaths previously thought to be suicide.

'Was this true?' I asked.

'There have been some, yes,' he confirmed.

This in itself was startling because I had assumed Platt had made up this fact to serve his own story. I asked the source could he make contact with the relevant parties on my behalf. 'I'm sorry, but I'm not going to do that,' he replied. 'Some of those families have already been caused pain. Like I said before, Geoff did have an active part in the investigation but his recall is fanciful and wrapped around a genuine case.

He was the PC on the murder squad tasked with picking up Kelly. Now he's put forward his version of the case and it is in direct contradiction of evidence.'

After listening to John Slater, I had tried to make sense of the competing narrative. The Kieran Kelly he'd represented wasn't the monster portrayed in the media, but a likeable pub-goer, more than capable of holding a conversation or breaking into a rerun of the Grand National. Slater's Kelly was a fantasist first and a killer second. It was his belief the Irishman's admissions were motivated by an appetite for notoriety. But the solicitor had nothing to back this up. Outside of the alleged murder claims, he could provide no other examples of Kelly the fantasist.

It wasn't like Kelly had told him he'd had trials for the football team he supported. Or that he came from a famous family in Ireland. There were no other examples, beyond the extreme claims of murder, that marked Kelly as a fantasist. And while he'd never felt threatened by Kelly, Slater reluctantly agreed that he'd seen enough and heard enough to make him believe his former client was capable of murder. That morning in 1983, when he heard on the radio that a man had been strangled to death in the cells of Clapham Police Station, his first thought was Kelly. Then there was the London Underground. While there *was* a record of Kelly attacking people on the network, no bodies had been identified.

Yet, yet, yet...

Officer A confirmed people had contacted the police in relation to family members who'd died under trains. They did so because they felt the deaths may in some way be connected with Kelly. Everywhere, it seemed, the story was in competition with itself and provided a different version of the truth.

It was a battle; like a dancing boxer trying to land an impossible knockout blow against his shadow opponent. Kelly, the cold killer with the affable personality; Kelly, the homosexual womanizer; Kelly, the London Underground serial killer with no confirmed kills on the underground. Not to mention the policeman with the credibility issue, yet one who had received a commendation for his work on the case.

Officer A revealed that both Platt and Brown had been spoken to by police, so too Slater, and that investigators were battling the same conflicting narrative. And amid the confusion and contradiction the central question remained – how many people did Kieran Kelly kill?

The investigation was still without a paper trail and the discovery of the remains on the site of Kelly's former home in Rathdowney, County Laois had yet to unearth an explanation. By early September 2016, the only significant development in relation to the skeletal remains and the wire noose was a verbal confirmation from a ranking officer connected with Portlaoise Garda Station that contact had been made with a Garda officer who'd policed that area of rural Laois in the 1990s.

Chapter 26

Lost Archive

Late September 2016 and an autumn chill blew off the Thames and into Kew in south-west London. On the yellowy, paved walkway leading up to The National Archives, water trickled out of a giant fountain, and outside the entrance a sign pointed upstairs towards the registration office. Registration took less than five minutes, but a computer notification indicated that access to the original Kelly court files from the Boyd and Fisher murder trials would take an hour and a half to retrieve. Both cases had been heard at the Old Bailey in London, in 1984. And after months of conversations, these files buried deep in the bowels of the building promised a factual narrative thus far absent from the Kelly story.

Months earlier, the courts service had rejected my requests to access the same file papers online because the period in question had yet to be digitized. This allowed the pursuit of Kelly's crime story to rest on the recollections of Geoff Platt, the considered recall of John Slater, and the confident presentation of a rap sheet, as remembered by the former detective inspector, Ian Brown.

From *The Huffington Post* to *The Irish Post*, the Kelly story was a murder puzzle of inaccurate news reports, fading hometown memories, hard-won facts surrendered by the security source and competing narratives. The case was anchored by the killings of Boyd and Fisher, yet the story of a prolific secret serial killer responsible for many more murders had been presented to the public and seized upon by both the media and the police because there was some substance to the claims. To what degree, made this story one that remained up for grabs.

Eventually, an online request to access the files had been granted and in an airy, grey-carpeted communal room in the National Archives, a notification sounded that the files were ready to view. They were assigned to a reading station, delivered by a clerical officer and arrived in a blue cover, worn flimsy by the march of time. Immediately, I noticed the file didn't have the name Kieran Kelly on the front, but the forename *Kieron*, which had then been scrubbed out and corrected so it read *Kiernan* Kelly. This forename was also incorrect.

Platt had said that sometimes Kelly used the forename Keith and the builder, Brian Sliman, had said that the accused always went by the name Ken. I wondered if this was a typo, or a series of clerical errors that inadvertently helped to bury what public records actually existed relating to the Kelly case. But then I had tried variations of Kelly's forename in the archive of the British Library and none unearthed any great trove of news reports.

There was also cause to question the almost minimal marking of Kelly's trial by the mainstream media in 1983. Was it possible the Kelly trial had been overshadowed by a bigger news story? Possibly the IRA's bombing campaign in Britain, which started to escalate around the time of his confessions, had meant the trial had bypassed the public consciousness.

In the quiet, imposing surrounds of the National Archives, confirmation had been given that the original court files for the William Boyd and Hector Fisher murder trials would be made available. However, only the appeals file had been delivered to the reading station. On the file index, the Boyd case was marked but the notes were nowhere to be found within the blue folder. There were only appeal notes related to the Fisher trial and the letter 'W' was marked beside the name of 'William Boyd' on the front cover index.

I brought the missing files to the attention of a staff member, who looked at the front cover carefully, turned it over, looked inside and observed that whatever had been dispatched to the reading station was all they had. Then he flipped the cover closed and looked at the index again. 'That W,' he said in reference to the circled letter beside Boyd's name on the index cover, 'must mean the case notes have been withheld.'

'Withheld by whom?' I asked.

'Possibly by The Ministry of Justice,' he replied. 'And I don't know why.'

Chapter 27

Date with the Old Bailey

On 11 July 1985, nearly two years after Kelly had been picked up for the robbery on Clapham Common that led to his confession of murder, a prison van edged out of the exit gates of Wormwood Scrubs Prison and beat a path towards central London and the Old Bailey. In the back of the van, Kieran Patrick Kelly sat sober and pensive, with his elbows on his knees and his wrists cuffed. He rocked gently in motion with the speeding van. Ahead, Court Number 1 of the Old Bailey prepared for the resumption of his trial.

'The Queen versus Kiernan [*sic*] Patrick Kelly'

This was the heading on the charge sheet that had been retrieved from the vaults of the National Archives. John Slater solicitor, Michael Beckman QC and a third colleague in the defence team, Francis Jones, might have waited inside Court Number 1 for their client to arrive. The team had lodged an appeal in the case and Kelly's appearance would soon reveal whether this appeal was successful or not. In Court Number 1, John Slater familiarized himself with a charge sheet he knew well:

'**Count One - Murder**

Kiernan [*sic*] Patrick Kelly on a day unknown between the 17th day of July 1975 and the 20th day of July 1975, murdered Hector John Fisher.

'**Count Two - Robbery**

Kieran Patrick Kelly on the 4th day of August 1983, robbed Walter Lawrence Bell of a ring.

'**Count Three - Murder**

Kiernan [*sic*] Patrick Kelly on the 4th day of August 1983 murdered William Boyd.'

According to the appeal notes on count three, the murder of Boyd, the jury had already found Kelly guilty of manslaughter. However, the meandering multiple murder admissions made by Kelly to detectives Ian Brown, Ray Adams, Andre Baker and others were nowhere to be seen.

The jury knew nothing of claims Kelly pushed his friend Christy Smith on to the tracks at Baker Street Station in 1953. Nothing of the trio of murder confessions from 1973, where Kelly detailed the stabbing to death of a man in Bournemouth, the beating to death of a homeless man in Shepherd's Bush, and another in Vauxhall. Nothing of the admissions to poisoning a man with prescription drugs behind a library in Tooting. Nothing of his acquittal for the murder of Edward Toal in Kennington Park in 1977. No sign of a claimed arson attack on a derelict building where he said a sleeping homeless man had been burned to death. The man who stumbled into the hospital in Peckham Rye and later died of cirrhosis of the liver didn't appear on the charge sheet either. Nor did the assisted suffocation of a man in Coronation Buildings near Vauxhall.

The jury would have been oblivious to all these admissions, known only to the detectives who worked the case, possibly Slater, Kelly's defence team and one or two others – all present in a court that had become synonymous in Ireland with the trials of those charged with IRA-related activity.

After the lengthy and often confusing interview of the Irishman in the smoke-filled room of Clapham Police Station, Kieran Patrick Kelly from Rathdowney in County Laois had been charged with robbery and two counts of murder. Somewhat unusually he'd been found guilty by a jury but on a reduced charge of manslaughter for the murder in the cells. But after originally confessing to the crimes, he was now pleading innocent.

When the prison van approached the Old Bailey, security pulled open the heavy gates at the entrance and the van swept into the grounds of the court. When the lock on the back door clinked open, Kelly might have glanced around as he climbed from the van. But here was no dissenting crowd of onlookers calling his name, no scrum of sharp-elbowed photographers jostling for a profile snap of this prolific executioner of murder and mayhem.

If the minimal media coverage was anything to go by, no one was too interested in a brutal double murder case, despite the case being heard in the spiritual centre of British justice. And that would only change when the rest of an alleged confession, that listed more than half-a-dozen murders according to Brown, and 'twenty-four serious crimes' according to the security source, was revealed decades later.

Based on information contained in the case notes and the testimony of key witnesses to the trial, it was possible to reconstruct scenes from Kelly's court appeal.

A uniformed Met police officer would have taken the defendant by the arm as he stepped from the van then escorted him through the building entrance and along the corridor towards Court Number 1. By then, the Honourable Mr Justice

Davies would have taken his place behind the bench, readying his papers as the court filled. On the floor of the court, John Slater, Michael Beckman and Francis Jones might have leaned in to talk in quiet conference. And the prosecution team of Mr M. Coombe and Mr T. Cassel would have sat close by. Also in the court throughout differing periods of the trial were Detective Inspector Ian Brown, Detective Superintendent Jestico, Detective Superintendent Andre Baker and Detective Constable McMillian.

During the trial, they would have heard a stoic and sober Kelly proclaim his innocence and listened with interest when he took the stand and told Justice Davies he'd been in Pentonville Prison the night Hector Fisher was beaten, stabbed and murdered.

The charge says the murder took place between 17 and 20 July, suggesting the prosecution didn't even know exactly when Fisher was murdered. This uncertainty around the date and time of death was played upon by the defence team. Because Kelly said he was in prison waiting to be released for another offence in the hours before Fisher was killed and there was no paper record that could prove or disprove this claim.

Back in 1975, investigators had taken over 280 statements on the Fisher case, among them one made by Kelly to a Detective Constable Clabby. The jury had waited with anticipation for the accused to take the stand. They'd spent days studying Kelly from their seats – a pensive, lean, middle-aged, former construction worker charged with a double murder. But it wouldn't have been until he took to the stand that the jurors could have made a human connection with the Irishman and the terrible crimes the state had charged him with.

They had listened to officers refer to statements made by Kelly in the interview room in Clapham Police Station, months earlier. How the accused had claimed to have been sleeping rough on the common for months. How he'd admitted to murdering Fisher because he believed he was 'a puff'.

But sober and under cross-examination from the prosecution team of Mr Coombe and Mr Cassel, Kelly denied all charges and denied ever knowing Fisher. The jurors in Court Number 1 heard claims from Kelly that it was the police who told him Fisher got 'cut' and mutilated when they picked him up for questioning in 1975. This is how he knew about the mutilation, not by the action of his own hand.

There was a line of witnesses but the pathologist, Professor Johnson, was called first. He gave a physical description of the victim, Fisher, as a man 5ft 4in tall and weighing a little over eight stone. Then, he listed the injuries inflicted on Mr Fisher. Court Number 1 heard that the victim suffered numerous injuries to the neck, head, chest, and defensive injuries to his left arm and right hand. There were twenty-one other injuries – twenty to the head and neck and one stab wound to the chest. Professor Johnson estimated there must have been twenty-eight blows altogether.

Of the twenty injuries to the head and neck, ten were categorized as blunt blows; ten as cuts or lacerations. The cut to Fisher's neck measured 5 inches long and it was Johnson's belief the blunt blows may have been caused by a whisky bottle. However, the jurors heard no evidence whatsoever in relation to claims the victim's genitals had been mutilated.

Significantly, however, Professor Johnson said he inspected Fisher's body at the scene and found three £5 notes in the right breast pocket of his jacket. There was also a sum of money in Fisher's back trouser pocket and the two amounts of money made a total of nearly £30 found on the victim. It was this previously suggested discovery of money that had helped tie Kelly to the murder scene. Though reading the case notes it struck me that the pathologist had not given an exact amount and that Brown was definite that they'd discovered two £20 notes, which didn't add up to £30.

Just how much was immaterial however. Kelly had made a statement to the DI and his fellow officers placing himself at the crime scene and claimed he'd left money on the body in a bid to confuse officers. This piece of information on its own did not make Kelly the murderer but, according to Brown, that there was a sum of money left on the body was something only the killer could have known.

A Mrs Turcus took to the stand. She told Justice Davies and the court she had seen Fisher the Monday before he was killed and that he was with an Irishman who she believed to be around 6ft tall, of stocky build and with a ruddy complexion. Next came the Timothys, a married couple who ran a fish shop near the Holy Trinity church in Clapham Common where Fisher's body was found. They knew Hector Fisher as a regular customer. They remembered him for his somewhat scruffy appearance and that he always seemed to be carrying plenty of money.

The last time they clapped eyes on the victim was two days before the Saturday on which Professor Johnson estimated Fisher was murdered. The coroner had been unable to fix a time of death to a date and this added weight to claims by the defence that Kelly was innocent. They said whatever information the accused knew was coincidental and picked up in conversations on the common.

Fisher's sister was called before the court. She revealed that her brother was once a flourishing businessman and that this was why he always carried large amounts of money. He once owned a successful printing business but after his wife died he'd struggled to cope with her loss and descended into depression and alcohol. This was new to me as Platt had said Fisher had got divorced, which again highlighted his propensity to get facts wrong. Fisher's sister said her brother drank in pubs on the Wandsworth Road and hung out with people her friends would have branded vagrants, dossers and winos. She reasoned that bereavement and addiction had thrust him into this world.

There were two musicians named in the archive files, a Mr Holt and a Mr Ayres, and the night before Fisher's body was found they said they saw him staggering about at 9pm, so drunk that he couldn't string two words together. Mr Ayres lived close to the common and told the court he'd got up early the next morning to catch a bus for a business trip. Upon leaving his house he noticed a figure slumped on a bench on the common, close to Holy Trinity church. He'd walked over to investigate and when he did, he realized it was the drunk man from the night before. But he was dead, and there was a deep gash in his head.

There was the curious testimony of a Mr Horan who'd taken to the witness stand to tell the court how, shortly after Fisher's body was discovered, he'd supplied Kelly with a change of clothes. He'd said that, in return, Kelly had given him a black shirt with stripes and a pair of dark trousers streaked with paint. He said he did not see any blood on the clothes but it would have been impossible to spot because the clothes Kelly had given him were so dirty.

In Court Number 1 of the Old Bailey, the witness statements appeared to pull the case back and forth between the defence and the prosecution. For the prosecution, potentially case-damaging descriptions of a man seen with Hector Fisher that didn't match the profile of Kieran Kelly had been made by more than one witness, and this was seized upon by the defence.

So too was the nature of some of the injuries suffered by the victim, in particular the supposed mutilation of Fisher's genitals. In the interview room in Clapham Police Station in 1983, Brown said Kelly told him and the investigation team that he'd stabbed Fisher in the bollocks. But no details of injuries inflicted on this part of Fisher's body were revealed to the jury because the pathologist told the court that they never happened.

This, along with the witness testimony of Mrs Turcus who described a tall, stocky Irishman of ruddy complexion, not a skinny Irishman of medium height, undermined the prosecution. Then there was the evidence of the shopkeeper who ran an off-licence close to the common. The uncertainty around his testimony was significant enough for the defence team of Beckman, Slater and Jones to lodge an appeal. And in July 1985, they'd reason to believe that Kieran Kelly would be acquitted, yet again.

Chapter 28

Appeal

Victor Pearson ran the off-licence in 5 Clapham Old Town. He worked there with his wife Anne, and one of his customers was a small, sometimes scruffy and slightly built middle-aged man whose regular order was a bottle of wine and half a bottle of White Horse Whisky. Mr Pearson didn't have a personal relationship with Hector Fisher. But through his dealings with him he'd come to know the man as someone who was courteous and polite, despite his appearance. Nor could the dutiful, law-abiding Mr Pearson have imagined that nearly ten years later, he'd become a key witness for the prosecution in a trial over the death of his former customer on Clapham Common.

Mr Pearson said he saw Fisher in the week beginning 7 July 1975. But this was a full ten days, or possibly even more, before he was found dead. Most of the time, Fisher visited the couple's off-licence alone. But on the night of 7 July – nearly two weeks before he was murdered – he came with another man who Mr Pearson remembered as being of stout build. The man had asked Fisher to buy him some English cider. Mr Pearson remembered because he was used to dealing with a sometimes intoxicated public late at night. This heightened his awareness. But he bagged up Fisher's order and the men left.

By 1984, Victor Pearson had left Clapham Common. He was still in the drinks trade, only now he ran an off-licence in Carshalton, south of London in Surrey. This was where he was paid a visit by a police clerk called Vera Bozic. She travelled from London with a folder containing two key pieces of evidence related to the Fisher trial. They were photographs. One was a profile shot of Kelly – craggy, drawn, sharp-featured. The other was that of Paul McManus, the man who had been arrested along with Kelly that August afternoon in 1983, when they'd robbed Walter Bell.

It had been McManus whose terrified shouts sounded about Clapham Police Station after he'd witnessed the murder of William Boyd in the cells. Bozic knew McManus had nothing to do with either the murder of Boyd or Fisher. But investigators wanted to test the retailer's description of the so-called 'stocky' man who'd visited his off-licence along with the victim before his murder. So Bozic presented the two images to him and waited for a reaction.

'That was definitely not the person referred to in the evidence,' said Pearson, pointing at the image of Kelly. Then he explained how, months later, he was paid a visit by the same 'stout' man. It was in the evening and the man had taken three flagons of cider off the shelf but he was short of money. He offered to bring back the empties to make up the difference. There was an argument, and the stout man left the shop with just two flagons of cider instead of three. Pearson told officers he didn't trust the man and that it wasn't the man in the picture. The physical description the shop owner provided didn't match the profile of Kelly, who was too tall, angular and lean to be considered stocky. Sharp, pointy, wiry – these were the adjectives people used again and again to describe Kelly. Not stocky.

This description cast doubt on the credibility of a prosecution case already challenged by the pathologist Professor Johnson's disclosure that Hector Fisher's genitals had in fact not been mutilated in the attack. Throughout the course of the trial, John Slater had come to the conclusion that Kelly was a fantasist who had concocted victims and crimes beyond those for which he was being tried in the Old Bailey – Fisher and Boyd.

The young solicitor believed his client had attached his name to deaths for which there were no bodies. Slater and Michael Beckman QC needed to seize upon the opportunity created by Pearson's uncertainty. Beckman approached Justice Davies with an unusual request. He and his team wanted to call Victor Pearson – who was key in the prosecution effort to convict Kelly – as a key witness for the defence. This was highly irregular and Justice Davies delved into the memory bank of his career in an attempt to recall any instance when a witness for the prosecution was called as a witness for the defence. In court he described it as 'unprecedented'. Beckman argued there were no property rights over the witness but the judge declined.

However, the approach from the defence added to a general feeling that Pearson was an unreliable witness to his own testimony. And the more doubt the defence could cast upon the case, the more difficult it would be for the prosecution to remove that feeling from the guts of the jury. Whichever way you looked at it, this uncertainty was good news for Kelly. But if the Kelly case was in danger of getting lost in the fog, Judge Davies sharpened the wandering focus of the Old Bailey with his summing up. 'I'm not the type of judge who can sit through a case and not form an opinion,' he opened. 'It would be a very cold fish who could do that. But the charge is this, that Keirnan [*sic*] Patrick Kelly murdered Hector John Fisher.

'Now, we know that the murder occurred on the dates of July 18th and 19th. And there is no dispute that Fisher was brutally killed that night, probably around midnight, you may think, on Clapham Common near the Holy Trinity church. Now the question for you to decide is – and the only question in the case is – whether you are sure that the defendant was the killer.

'He denies it and denied it under oath in the witness box. The witness told police previously that he had drink taken at the time of the interview. If I can just take a moment to point you to a passage of text where Mr Kelly was asked: "How many times did you stab him?" And his reply was: "I don't know I had a good drink on me."

'You the jury, if you feel that alcohol diminished Kelly's intent, then you should downgrade the charge to manslaughter. But it must be pointed out the prosecution's case really depends on the defendant's confessions because he admitted it more than once to the police. Mr Kelly said the police had not obtained the admissions out of him. And there is nothing to suggest the police recorded anything that was not untrue; not the slightest scrap of evidence to suggest Mr Kelly had anything to be frightened of. He repeated his admissions in the presence of his solicitor.

'What, of course, is the $64,000 question is were the confessions true? If the confessions were true then you might be quite right to think that Mr Coombe of the prosecution *was* quite right and the defendant *was* guilty of murder. Furthermore, you do not need a lot of evidence to conclude that there is a world of difference, shall we say, between the grounds of Buckingham Palace and Clapham Common at night.

'There is enough evidence for you to conclude, if you do not know it as a matter of general knowledge, that it is a haunt of people of the type I have been describing and no doubt violence often breaks out there. That is something you should bear in mind. Mr Beckman called them "the dregs of society". People who would not shrink from using violence towards others, which seems to suggest that the deceased was in the company of others – who, if I may follow my rather fanciful reference – are people you would not expect to find strolling on the lawn of Buckingham Palace at a garden party.'

Citing the prosecution, Justice Davies said: 'Mr Coombe said the defendant is the only person capable of killing Mr Fisher and Kelly is the only person who made a reliable admission to it.'

Then Judge Davies reflected on Fisher's lifestyle and expressed his regret about the decline of the once-successful businessman; a decline that had been explained in stark terms. The victim had come to a sorry end, he suggested, not just because of an inability to cope with the loss of his wife, or his relationship with alcohol, but because of sexual desires that lured him to the common in the hope he'd meet other men.

'The pathologist, Professor Johnson, said that in the past the unfortunate Mr Fisher had indulged in homosexual activities,' said the judge. 'There is no evidence to suggest that they were illegal homosexual activities,' he added. 'And you may realize that people who indulge in that behaviour may find themselves mixed up with people who are violent and indeed sometimes merciless. One may say I have been rather unkind with respect to the defendant about the late gentleman, but whatever depths he had sunk to, he was a human being and a fellow citizen of yours and mine and his killing is just as much a crime as if he had been a reputable person within the City of London.'

The crime's sexual undertone had been given as a motive by Kelly, who had told Detective Inspector Ian Brown he'd killed Fisher because the businessman had made an unwanted advance and 'wanted his arse'. In 2016, Platt had consistently progressed a press narrative that portrayed Kelly as homophobic, someone who encouraged sexual advances from men, which he then used as justification to kill. Time and again, Platt said that their frequent journeys to and from London courts and Wormwood Scrubs Prison featured conversations about Kelly's sexuality. The murky subtext to some of the murders was the bubbling up of Kelly's suppressed homosexuality; that these murders were in some way motivated by the destruction of his own soul, by his own self-loathing.

Reading the case notes, I wondered whether a sexual arrangement was the reason why Kelly and Fisher were sitting on the bench together, behind Holy Trinity church, that 1975 night in Clapham Common. Was Fisher feeding Kelly's alcohol habit in return for sexual favours? Or was Kelly a willing participant in some kind of sexual relationship? Maybe it was the case that Fisher's homosexuality became a convenient explanation. One that helped Kelly square off his murder with his own conscience.

But Kelly hadn't just detailed an act of murder. He'd confessed to mutilating Fisher's genitals with a broken whisky bottle. It was this element of the crime that unnerved homeless men and women on the common. Daytime whispers of mutilation screamed into their subconsciousness when darkness fell.

Eight years later, Kelly confessed to the murder, but also injuries never found on the victim's body. The most distressing element of the case had been rendered redundant by the pathologist's report and the defence appeared at pains to point out that, while Kelly admitted to the injuries, that didn't mean he killed Fisher. It was possible it was someone else.

'Well, the defendant told the police that he cut the man about the bollocks and that's why Beckman used that word in ringing terms yesterday,' declared Judge Davies. 'But we now know there is absolutely no evidence to back up this claim. So, there are three different types of explanation here,' he continued. 'Some made up, some things he said he learned from police and some he put down to dosser gossip.

'The prosecution points out that there are matters in the confession that only Mr Kelly could have known. And you do not admit to murder unless you have done it or unless you are a crank who wants to attract publicity. This was what the prosecution submitted. Throughout the case, I and the court have heard things I know not to be true, but the question I'd put to the jury is, are they substantially true? If the answer is yes, then there is no doubt that the defendant is the killer.'

Chapter 29

The Verdict

The voice of the clerk of the court cut through a rising hum of chatter in the Old Bailey to ask the jury a question. Had they reached a decision upon which they had all agreed? The foreman of the jury stood up. 'No,' he replied.

Judge Davies craned his neck, Kieran Kelly shifted anxiously in his seat, and Ian Brown and his fellow officers, seated at the back of the court, might have exchanged worried glances. The floor of the court hummed again with chattering voices. BANG-BANG-BANG, sounded Judge Davies' gavel. The court fell quiet again.

'MEMBERS OF THE JURY HAVE YOU REACHED A DECISION ON WHICH AT LEAST *TEN* OF YOU HAVE AGREED?' added the clerk, this time in a louder voice.

'YES,' replied the foreman of the jury.

'On the charge of murder. DO YOU FIND THE DEFENDANT GUILTY OR NOT GUILTY?' asked the clerk.

'GUILTY.'

BANG-BANG-BANG went the gavel again.

'IS THAT A VERDICT FROM ALL OF YOU, OR JUST THE MAJORITY?'

'MAJORITY,' said the foreman, raising his voice to compete with the noise. 'ELEVEN AGREED TO THE VERDICT AND ONE DISSENTED.'

Sitting on the floor of the court, Kelly was no stranger to the hammer of justice falling against him. He'd been in and out of prison since the 1950s. But this verdict was different. The jury had returned a verdict of manslaughter in the case of the death of William Boyd in the cells, but found Kelly guilty of murdering Hector Fisher. In 1985, this carried a tariff of life in prison. This verdict meant that Kelly would never live another free day ever again.

When the chatter dissipated in Court Number 1, the clerk repeated what he'd just heard from the jury but in a quieter voice. 'So, eleven found him guilty of murder and one dissented,' he confirmed. The foreman nodded and the defence team sat in quiet conference. John Slater, Michael Beckman QC and Francis Jones were already planning to lodge another challenge on the grounds that Judge Davies had failed to facilitate *their* calling of Pearson as a witness for the defence.

The one – and possibly only – card they'd left to play was the presentation of a stocky killer with a ruddy profile that contradicted Kelly's angular features. But whether it *was* Kelly that Pearson saw with Fisher in 1983, and on another occasion when 'a man' entered his shop in Clapham Old Town, this contest of competing descriptions was over. The defence decided against lodging another appeal. Kelly's admissions of murder, his inability to provide a cast-iron alibi, the contradictions he made under cross-examination, and the evidence he provided 'that only the killer could have known' had sealed his fate.

On count three – the murder of William Boyd – Kelly had previously entered a plea of not guilty. The jury had found him not guilty of murder but guilty of manslaughter. They'd also found him guilty by unanimous decision on count two – the robbery of Walter Bell.

Judge Davies got ready to pass sentence. On count three, Kelly had been sentenced to life in prison. On count two, he was sentenced to three years. So in July 1985, the court stood and listened as Kelly received an automatic life term for the murder of Hector Fisher, and the cuffed prisoner was whisked from the court to a waiting prison van to start a jail sentence that would run for the rest of his natural life.

In the months that followed, Kelly made a written appeal through his solicitors in respect of the Fisher verdict. It came to nothing and the Irish prisoner spent time incarcerated in a number of UK prisons before he was transferred to Frankland Prison in Durham, in the north of England. According to Platt, Kelly spent much of the rest of his life locked up in isolation, separated from the general prison population. It was impossible to determine if this was true or not.

Kieran Kelly died in 2001 in Frankland Prison. He was 71. But the press office for the prison service of England refused to provide any details related to his incarceration, or facilitate a request to visit the prison. Nagging features remained – the conflicting profile descriptions of the killer; the unfounded claims of mutilation presented by Kelly, the fantasist; the carelessness of administrators who registered the defendant under three different forenames: Kieran, Kiernan and Kieron.

In addition, Officer A was unable to offer any explanation as to why case files related to the manslaughter of William Boyd had been marked 'W', possibly 'withheld', in the National Archives in Kew. Was it the case that there was information contained within that the police didn't want the public to see? Or was the disappearance of the file just an innocent clerical error that unwittingly added more mystique to efforts to discover the truth in this case?

Chapter 30

Where are All the Bodies?

Why wasn't Kelly tried for all his other murder admissions? Why was the ratio of convictions to alleged admissions so disproportionate? The Kelly investigation, like the Kelly story, was a numbers game that continued to tax the police. Meanwhile the former policeman, Geoff Platt, continued to fuel the story with his running total of Kelly murders. By early autumn 2016, that figure was holding at thirty-one. But even the double-digit murder tally the former DI Ian Brown claimed Kelly confessed to jarred with the murder and manslaughter the Irish labourer was successfully tried and convicted of.

By the time of his appeal in July 1985, the 55-year-old Irishman had already been tried and acquitted for the 1977 murder of Edward Toal and acquitted for the attempted murder of Francis Taylor at Tooting Bec Underground Station in 1982. The Scotsman, Gordon McMurray, had decided against advancing a similar charge against Kelly after he'd ended up on the tracks at Oval Underground Station. But there was still the admission of murder against a man Kelly named as Christy Smith from 1953, and a trio of murder admissions from 1973, comprising a stabbing in Bournemouth, a bricking to death and burial of Scotch Jack in a Vauxhall basement, and the beating to death of a man in Shepherd's Bush.

According to Brown, Kelly had also confessed to the assisted suffocation of a man in Coronation Buildings, Vauxhall in 1976 by force-feeding him alcohol and allowing him to choke on his vomit. Brown said there was also evidence that backed up claims Kelly poisoned a man he called Mickey Dunne behind a library in Tooting in 1982. These admissions formed the spine of Kelly's investigation. So it didn't stack up that the lesser charge of robbery of Walter Bell in Clapham figured on Kelly's day of reckoning in the Old Bailey when the defendant had apparently confessed to at least nine other murders. And why were the press so seemingly disinterested in Kelly's murder trial?

In August 1983, the BBC's morning news bulletin had reported the strangulation of William Boyd in the cells of Clapham Police Station. But this story had largely failed to register with the red top tabloid newspapers on Fleet Street. The manslaughter of Boyd and murder of Fisher were little more than dismissible briefs on a roll of microfilm in the British Library. In July 1985, around the time of Kelly's appeal, the press were focusing on security stories sparked by the IRA bombing of the Grand Hotel in Brighton the previous October. That attack targeted the then British Prime Minister Margaret Thatcher and left five dead, injuring dozens more.

Following the commencement of his trial and later, his sentencing, Kelly had returned to Wormwood Scrubs Prison to begin his life sentence, and DI Brown had moved on to Scotland Yard's specialist C4 Unit in search of the missing gold from the notorious Brink's-Mat robbery at Heathrow Airport.

News of a failed appeal by Kelly's defence team must have been received with apathy by investigators. Brown and his team had returned two life sentences for a manslaughter charge in the case of Boyd and a murder charge in the case of Fisher. Kelly's history of violence that purportedly reached back beyond his first term in Broadmoor in 1969 had been marked with a full stop. To Brown and his colleagues, Kelly was the dangerous, violent criminal who strangled a man to death with a pair of knotted socks in a police cell and stabbed and bludgeoned to death a failed businessman for the hell of it.

And that had only been the tip of the iceberg. Multiple, cavalier acts of violence that ended in murder were a hallmark of this case. That he'd succeeded in murdering with his bare hands was one of the things about his story that set it apart. Meanwhile claims he killed and attempted to kill on two separate occasions on the tube earned him the nickname – the London Underground Serial Killer.

But most interesting was what set his victims apart from the rest of society. That they were drunken vagrants, social pariahs – in many instances shunned even by their own family, never mind wider society. And they were all men. This was reason enough for Kelly to attack and kill. And this was the core reason, according to investigators, that the Irishman didn't face trial for these admissions.

Chapter 31

Justice Takes Investment

Ian Brown took a hit from his electronic cigarette, shrugged and repeated his answer of the question he'd just been asked: why did the Kelly story attract such little media attention? 'Because they were tramps,' he said, easing his frame back to rest on the bonnet of an old motor parked in the overflow car park of his golf club in Kent. It was another brilliantly sunny afternoon in the early autumn of 2016 and a green ride-on lawnmower zipped past, breaking the silence as it bore down on another fairway. Standing beneath a tree canopy in the quiet of the Kent countryside, the former detective inspector looked into the distance and shook his head, almost in resignation.

After a thirty-three-year hiatus it was more than a little peculiar to be here answering questions about the Kelly case, and why, despite its seriousness, the case had never penetrated the public consciousness. 'It was because they were tramps and alcoholics,' he shrugged again. Tramps that slept out on the common, and tramps who died for a variety of reasons. 'If they died of a head injury then someone might assume that they'd fallen over stone drunk.

'Kelly was a tramp murderer. He hated tramps – he was one. He hated alcoholics – he was one. And he hated homosexuals, though, I don't remember Kelly saying if he was one or not. I don't know if Kelly found it cleansing,' he continued.

'But there was a bravado to his confession. It was like he was *proud* of it.'

In the car park, a key turned in the ignition of a car engine and the sound of gravel being crunched under slowly moving tyres accompanied the departing vehicle. Brown frowned and suggested that some of the deaths Kelly confessed to – well, they'd chosen to treat them with less rigour *because* the victims lived on the margins of society. They were lost people communities didn't miss. People who hid their shame and identity behind made-up monikers and nicknames. This made them difficult to identify. And difficult to identify with.

Some didn't have families. Others never expected to return home to their families. They were without profile and without the kind of responsibilities that now make people easy to track down – for instance, there were no mortgage repayments, which would require a bank account.

Outpourings of grief didn't accompany the death of homeless street drinkers. It was a curious fact of life that the media and the public didn't care so much for stories about dead tramps. Not Edward Toal, found strangled to death on a cold slab of stone in Kennington Park. Not William Boyd, a person whose only crime was vagrancy but whose punishment was death. These were people who begged on street corners, who jumped the gates of London Underground stations to ride the line in winter just to stay warm. They were people who, incredibly, slept slumped over taut ropes stretched between two points in the yards of homeless shelters.

It was an environment where vagrants, drunks and rough sleepers often turned on each other. Possibly, there were more murders and they too would have gone unrecorded. The victims were people who picked through bins to find food, who fell asleep on the coldest of winter nights to never waken again. They died of acute alcohol poisoning. And, sometimes, died at the hands of their peers.

Misadventure.

Hypothermia.

Overdoses.

It was difficult to establish whether a homeless person had been murdered or not and there was no great rush to resolve these crimes higher up the police chain of management. In fact, the absence of public outrage granted the police a pass they'd never be gifted if Judge Davies' respectable 'City banker' turned up dead on London's streets.

But this story's lack of public penetration was significantly less important than the pursuit of justice. More than indifference for those who lived and died in this societal subculture, the Kelly case failed to register in the public consciousness because police management made a choice *not* to pursue the full breadth of Kelly's confession, according to former DI Brown. This was despite Brown's admission that they'd established a strong trail of evidence to follow. However, once Brown and his team had Kelly for the murders of Boyd and Fisher, their superiors were satisfied and the will to pursue the rest of the Irishman's confession subsided.

In 1984, the tariff on a life sentence was such that no matter how many more murders the police proved, Kelly would still see out the rest of his natural life behind bars. What extra they might do, what extra resources they might use, what extra money they might spend, it would not add a single minute to Kelly's sentence.

In the crimes against Boyd and Fisher, investigators possessed the kind of evidence that allowed them to build strong cases against the defendant. If Kelly was sentenced for a double murder then he was going down for life. Investing further resources to prove cases that the police and the public cared little for was not a dispensation that would have been readily granted to Brown by his commanding officers. They could throw a load of resources at the case, sanction overtime, and open up investigations on multiple fronts. But that wasn't going to add to Kelly's sentence. He was still going to end up with the same life tariff he received for killing Boyd and Fisher.

'He almost certainly did what he told us he did,' said Brown, standing up from the car bonnet in the golf club and taking a deep breath. 'But you have to remember that Kelly was mad. Like I said, as far back as 1969, Kelly committed a robbery in south-east London, went to a house and when the woman answered, he rushed in with knives, tied her up and robbed her. He was detained under the Mental Health Act and was sent to Broadmoor, the home of the criminally insane. He stayed for two years and they realized there was not much they could do with him and so they released him in 1971 and he ran amok for the next fifteen years.

'But the admissions of murder that he made and that we traced, were exactly as Kelly said. When we found Scotch Jack in the house in Vauxhall, he'd multiple head wounds and why would you suspect murder when a man has fallen down twenty steps into a basement? Kelly said it was him and he couldn't have known about it otherwise.

'Listen, you can't give someone five life sentences when they only have one life,' he shrugged again, before sitting back down on the car. 'Once you get to the point that you have him on two murders and the sentence is going to be life in prison, then there is no point, financially or otherwise, in carrying on. That's why the other admissions were never pursued.'

Chapter 32

A Seed of Doubt

Sitting in his office on the Upper Richmond Road, John Slater smiled an apology and explained that he had a pending appointment. There was only so much time available to reflect on the Kelly case. He'd spent his life as a solicitor and absolutely he accepted there was no motivation for the police to pursue Kelly's other murder claims; that the fixed tariff of 'life' his client received could not be lengthened by additional convictions, no matter what the number. It wouldn't have affected his sentence. 'There would be no incentive on police to try and get him for ten,' he reasoned, 'because of the time it would take to form separate murder squads to go after all these claims.'

The upstairs office had fallen quiet, the clock ticked and then Slater's simmering annoyance bubbled up. He was aggrieved at the re-emergence of the Kelly story after so many years; annoyed at Geoff Platt's self-promotion to the role of principle witness and the revisionism that had led the police to reopen the case. 'Platt was a bag-carrier,' he said with a dismissive wave. 'He was not directly involved. When I met him once I felt he saw it [getting the story out there] as a way of making money. As lots of his version is personal knowledge he got certain things wrong and I feel he got dates wrong.'

Slater's opinion was not a privately held position. It was true that the story had been widely reported, but the penetration would have been far greater had it not been for Platt's conflicting testimony. It served to undermine a case worthy of greater scrutiny and scared off large sections of the press.

'What I do find surprising is that, as a bag-carrier, he was not involved in a senior position and he is trying to carry the weight as if he is a principle character,' he continued.

'Do you think Kieran Kelly has been misrepresented in the media?' I asked.

'Yes,' he replied defiantly. 'Yes, I do.'

'Do you feel aggrieved because of that?' I added.

'I think it's unfortunate that Geoff Platt presented *this* story and it's unhelpful,' he said. 'We'll probably never get to the bottom of it. And it's revived unpleasant memories for people who have lost people who have fallen under tube trains.' He paused for a moment. 'I just don't think it's helpful,' he added with more firmness. 'And I'm not sure where it is leading. It's wasting public money over an inquiry and a waste of police time. Let the historians do that and not waste public money.

'I think it is unfortunate, that police reaction. And that the commissioner of the police, Hogan-Howe, has called for an inquiry and I don't think he thought through where it was going and less inquiries are better than more.' Slater took a breath.

'Never mind the crimes he only confessed to. Are you still unsure about the convictions?' I wondered.

He raised his eyebrows.

'Why?' I pressed.

'Because of the nature of some of the allegations,' he said. 'Kelly said he stabbed him [Fisher] through the bollocks. That was the rumour going around and he wasn't...and I think Kelly picked up from those rumours and I still have doubts. I don't know.

'All I can say about Clapham Police Station and Boyd is that he was convicted of it. Three went into the cell and two came out and it is quite clear the chap was strangled and either Kelly or the other chap had done it and I would be surprised if it was the other chap. But I have to accept that he was convicted of manslaughter in the police station (and I never quite understood how the jury got to that conviction of manslaughter, by the way) and certain features of the Fisher case, well, he may have got them from reports that were inaccurate.'

'And the other crimes he confessed to but wasn't convicted of?' I asked.

'The police presented a fair case,' continued Slater. 'He was found guilty and the police acted professionally. But if you open the Kelly file, you will see a conviction for manslaughter and a conviction for murder. There is nothing to do with the underground, not twelve, sixteen, twenty-four or whatever many murders.'

The meandering pursuit of Kelly's murder rate was a wasted journey according to a solicitor who still appeared to be acting with admirable professional responsibility on behalf of his deceased client. But this feeling wasn't a hunch. John Slater hadn't been swayed in his assessment because he found his former client to be pretty agreeable on a personal level. No, the reason why he'd cause to doubt Kelly's capacity to murder at the rate reported was rooted in a fact that had not been reported. It was a fact that still troubled him decades later.

'As I said before, Kelly was a fantasist, and the reason why the police did not pursue him or charge him for all the other admissions was because he admitted to one, and the police actually discovered he was in prison at the time the murder was committed. That threw doubt over all the other admissions he had made.'

Chapter 33

False Ceiling

Brian Sliman lived on a quiet road near the River Thames and between the train stations of Putney and Wandsworth Town in south-west London. After his startling disclosure that he'd employed Kelly for four years, the Irish builder had committed to try and find someone else he had both worked with and who remembered 'Ken' Kelly. But sitting in his kitchen on this weekday evening, months after that first conversation in the pub, he explained that he'd been unable to trace anyone. 'I've been trying to think who I might get a hold of who would know more than I would about Ken,' he said clearly frustrated. 'And sure every one of them is dead – at least thirty I employed around that time are all dead.'

Interestingly however, there was one person sat in the rear kitchen of his terraced house near the rail line who had met Kelly — the builder's son, Mark. And though he was only a child at the time, *his* reaction to the emergence of Platt's story in 2015 echoed that of his father's. 'Is it true?' he asked, in what had by now become the investigation's key question. 'I met Ken when I was a boy. And I only have positive memories of helping him clean the van or whatever. I don't remember anything negative about him at all.'

Both father and son then drifted into conversations about Kelly, which allowed a greater insight into the

146

convicted killer and offered again an alternative insight into his persona. Lighting a cigarette, Brian Sliman steered the conversation back to one of the first jobs he completed with Kelly, not long after their memorable introduction outside the building site in Balham. Again, the location was Brixton – an area of London that would become their beat – and they were replacing a gutter on a three-storey property.

'The only way to do it was to go through the attic, take the slates off from the inside and punch a hole out of the roof,' he recalled. 'I knew we'd have to create a harness and abseil down to the gutter, but I didn't know Ken at all then. Remember, it was still in my head, him punching holes in the galvanizing. So I said: "Listen, I'll feed the rope in and out to you, you go. I've threaded the rope around the chimney and around a beam. Even if I have a heart attack and the rope slips, you will only fall a few feet and the rope will save you."

'Ken took off down the roof like a mountain climber. He was skinny, wiry and it wasn't easy to work in those conditions – he was dangling off the side of this building from the rope, fixing the gutter with these clips. At the halfway point he wanted to come in because he said the ropes were cutting into him, but I said: "If you come in now you won't go back out," and I persuaded him to stay put.

'When he did come in, there were these awful black marks from where the rope had been cutting into his body and I knew then there was a real hardness to him. But at the same time, there were other sides to Ken. He was always well turned out, never swore and he didn't like when people used derogatory terms about women, even if he didn't know the woman. People called him Nosey Kelly but I never noticed his nose, to be honest.

'A woman he was with had three kids and I never saw her but I met the kids and they were lovely. After her, he moved in with the woman in Brixton – the mother of the daughter Ken attacked in Reading. I do know that every kid he ever met liked him. I liked him, but not in the way you think in terms of as a friend, but because he was able to do the work I wanted him to do. When we finished he'd go off his way and I'd go off mine.'

Sliman said he didn't like to socialize with Kelly because alcohol made him volatile, although sometimes it was unavoidable. 'We were in a job in Folkestone once,' he recalled. 'It was a Sunday evening and coming home the lads wanted a drink. I was driving so I said we'd stop for one, two at most. We pulled into this place and there was a guy behind the bar. He must have been 6ft 9in tall. He was a big fella. I mean *big*. And there was a woman working behind the bar too and Ken was looking at her and he'd a pint in him now so I was watching him because I knew what he was like and didn't want him to get too pissed. The next time I looked he was on his second pint and he was still looking at the woman again and then he calls her – but by name.

'She turns around and this big fella turns around too and puts his arm around her and then Ken says: "You look different to when you were younger and you used to go around Brixton with your knickers in your hand as a child!" There was a moment when nothing happened and I was thinking we are going to get killed. And then the woman laughed. It turned out Ken had known her father and uncle. But that was the type of thing he'd do and he'd have done that if there were twenty boxers in the bar. He'd say anything.'

Sliman said this recklessness became a feature of their working relationship, until an incident on the south coast of England brought it to an abrupt end. Their final job together was a house restoration in Rye and he recalled how he collected a hungover Kelly from Clapham and they drove to the job, an old house that belonged to an older lady. The building was split into three different landings and it was Kelly's job to clear the furniture from the third floor. But a couple of hours after they started, Kelly had disappeared – along with a sizeable lump of money from the homeowner's purse.

Sliman was certain she'd made a mistake. Ken wouldn't do that to him. Their relationship had been soldered tight by a thousand jobs across the city. He took off in search of Kelly, double-parking on nearby streets and storming through a series of cafes and pubs where he enquired if anyone had seen a man matching his colleague's description.

In a pub close to Rye train station, he got a positive identification from a barman who had served someone fitting Kelly's description before the man left to catch a train back to London. Sliman parked by Rye Station and waited and half an hour later, Kelly appeared. 'I told him he had to come back,' said Sliman. 'That if he didn't come back, then we wouldn't be able to clear it up. "I'm not coming back," Kelly said. "I'm not well. I'm going home." I told him we had to go back. Otherwise it will be me and the other guys getting the blame. He still said no and he was nearly crying, but I said: "Dead or alive, we're going back."'

When they returned to the house there was a police car parked outside and one of the coppers took Sliman to one side. 'He told me that £300 was missing and I emptied my pockets for him to see and I nearly had £300 on me, myself. But I always carried a lot of cash to buy lead and that.' The officer explained that he couldn't force Kelly to empty his pockets but they agreed that when they went back inside, Sliman would volunteer to put his money on the table and then tell the other workers on the job to empty their pockets too. 'I said: "Come on now lads, we'll all put our money out on the table."

'Ken had no choice. He turned out his pockets but he'd broken down the £300 into smaller denominations. It was all fivers and tenners, but it was close enough to £300. I said to Ken: "Tell me, did you do it or not?" He continued to deny it but the police arrested him. They brought him out to the car, but the woman's purse was still missing. She didn't really care that much about the money, it was the other things that were in the purse.

'I said to Ken: "Listen once you get into that car and go, the chance of resolving this is gone." I told him that it was me

149

who was going to suffer out of it, not the woman. I was doing an awful lot of work around Belgravia then and money going missing from a house would have been the end of me. But still he refused to own up to what happened.

'I walked out with him to the police car. They put him in the back and they were just about to close the door when I said: "Ken, c'mon now, you owe it to me to sort this out. Once the car door closes, I'm finished." And right then, at the last minute, he admitted he done it. Burst into tears like a child.

'He said that on the way up the stairs he had poked his head around an open door and spotted a handbag open on the floor. There was a purse sticking out and he took it from the bag. On the landing of the house, Ken opened the purse and discovered £300. He put the roll of cash in his pocket and threw the empty purse up on to an old cabinet that was above head height on the landing of the old house.

'He broke down crying – more out of temper – and the police took him away. But the thing was, I could see what happened. Ken had been around houses with me for years and had never stolen anything, and he would have had loads of opportunities. But on this morning, he was hungover, walked into the wrong room with a carpet on his shoulder, saw the money in the purse and grabbed it. The thing was, I actually paid his bail bond.

'It wasn't long after that incident with the money in Rye that someone came to me and said they'd heard the story about Mad Ken, that he'd been arrested over something in Clapham Common. A gay man was killed and they arrested him for it, but the next thing I heard they let him go. Then, it came up again years later that he was picked up for twelve murders – but I dismissed that until you mentioned it and I was dumbfounded really.

'Had this never happened and someone walked up to me and asked me about Ken, then I would have said he was a bit of a bollocks really, but there was clearly a good side to him.

Drink was the one thing that would send him over the edge. That's when the red mist would come down.

'I remember about a year later,' added Sliman. 'I stopped into a pub, Jack Beard's in Tooting. I was stood at the bar and I felt like someone was looking over. When I glanced across, Ken was there by the far wall. He was looking at me – not in an aggressive way – and I just looked back at him and then walked out of the pub. And that was the last time I saw him.'

Chapter 34

Murder in Someone Else's Name

John Slater wasn't the only one troubled by the death of a man in Coronation Buildings opposite Vauxhall Park in 1976. Investigating officers found themselves challenged by Kelly's admission that he suffocated an unnamed man in a flat occupied by a person he named as Paddy Kelly. The flat was a well-known drinking den and Kieran Kelly told Ian Brown and his team that he'd forced drink down the man's throat until the man started to vomit. Then he stood and watched as he choked to death.

Kelly remembered the date. It was 15 April. Only no one was brought in for questioning. According to Brown, when the verdict was returned it concluded the man had choked on his own vomit. The likely cause of death was misadventure.

Like many of Kelly's other admissions, the story sounded thin, but detectives logged the date and details and to their surprise, they found a match. Enquiries revealed that an incident, almost identical in every way to the one Kelly described, happened in a flat in Coronation Buildings in Vauxhall on the same date – 15 April 1976. The thing was, according to Officer A, Kelly was locked up in Wandsworth Prison that night, serving a two-year sentence. 'He couldn't have left the confines of the prison to commit the murder,' he said. 'The detectives interviewed others present in the flat on the night in question and none remembered Kelly being present.'

* * *

It was now almost eighteen months since Geoff Platt's story of a secret serial killer whose crimes were never properly investigated was brought to the attention of the public and Britain's most senior policeman, Sir Bernard Hogan-Howe. Months previously, Officer A had revealed that a team from the British Transport Police and the Met were working through a crime list linking Kelly with twenty-four serious offences. Included on that list was the murder in Coronation Buildings in Vauxhall in 1976.

Officer A had also confirmed that conversations had taken place between the police, solicitor John Slater, investigators Ian Brown and Andre Baker, as well as Platt. 'John Slater *did* use the word fantasist and that Kelly admitted to a lot,' he said. 'And there was a view among investigators that Kelly would admit to an awful lot of things,' he conceded.

But Officer A speculated that because of the defendant's unreliability, his confessing to a murder he couldn't possibly have committed would have been a big concern for both the police and the prosecution at Kelly's trial. 'This would throw doubt on the Kelly case overall,' he said. 'But of course, this is just a theory. I don't know whether that's the case or not. But they could actually prove that Kelly was in Wandsworth Prison at the time. So he clearly could not have committed *that* offence.'

Then, during our telephone call, he started paging through what could only have been Kelly's case notes, shooting out information at random. 'The one with the body in the basement of the building in Vauxhall – that was knocked down and they built a huge block of flats on top of it,' he said. 'There was a man supposedly underneath there. But with no evidence of any murder existing, they were never going to knock a block of flats down to look for him.

'There were other ones, where Kieran Kelly refers to a fellow drinker [Mickey Dunne] he said he murdered, and how he did it was he poured drink down his throat and stood on his chest so he swallowed it all. And that he died a couple of days later as a result of that. Well, he did die after this supposed incident. Kieran Kelly said he was responsible for the murder, but then the pathologist said the man died of cirrhosis of the liver, so there is a conflict there in terms of how he came to have died.'

For investigators, that death was impossible to decipher, he said. But some of the others were easier to determine. 'They had access to Kelly's recorded confession,' said Officer A. 'And one of the cases that stuck out in my mind was Kelly's claim he stabbed a man to death in Bournemouth. But both at the time and in recent years, officers were unable to find any evidence of someone who died of stab wounds in Bournemouth in 1973.'

The source also disclosed that police had since dropped all enquiries brought about by people who'd got in touch following Platt's revelations; revelations that had given them cause to believe that their loved ones didn't die of suicide, but had been pushed to their death on the Northern Line. Platt had listed this figure at seven and Officer A speculated that these families might have got in touch more in hope than expectation.

But there was no doubt that the evidence that suggested Kelly's innocence was beginning to grow. 'Some people – not many – got in touch and said: "My husband is said to have taken his own life and was he one of the ones who was thrown on the tracks?"' said Officer A. 'But some of them are around 1985 and Kelly was in prison at that point,' he added.

'All in all,' he sighed, 'Kelly indicated that he was involved in about ten incidents. And of the ten that were investigated by the Met, they could charge for some of those offences and not the others.' Even if Kelly had been responsible for some of the deaths, one problem remained for Officer A and those who investigated this case before him. 'It's very hard to prove a murder of a tramp unless someone's seen it.'

Chapter 35

No Right of Reply

Information may now have been leaking out from behind police lines in the UK, but in Ireland there was still no response from the Gardaí in relation to the remains discovered on the site of Kelly's former home. Three months of emails and more than a dozen contact requests had led to nothing. At a divisional level in Ireland, Gardaí had been made aware that an investigation of sorts was being conducted by two separate police forces in the UK – The Met and the British Transport Police. It had been made clear that Kelly's time in Ireland may be worthy of scrutiny too, considering a skeleton was discovered at the former County Laois home of the twice-convicted killer.

Claims a wire noose had been discovered around the neck of the skeletal remains were also brought to the attention of the Gardaí. And that this may also be significant because both Edward Toal and William Boyd had been garroted with a length of rope and knotted socks respectively. Attacks on victims' air passages were a recurring theme in the crimes that Kelly had been tried for and the ones still being looked into.

According to the security source, Platt had added this discovery to his body count, and despite new evidence, it still felt like a reach to attach the body in the garden to his then adolescence. Yet it remained an annoying fact that while the family left the town in apparent haste, Kelly's mother returned every year on some pilgrimage.

I had been reluctant to get in touch with the Gardaí's national press office because I figured it would slow the response time. However, by October 2016, when the enquiries in Ireland had no place left to go, I made contact.

01/10/2017

To whom it concerns

For the last months, I've been researching the case history of Kieran Patrick Kelly from Rathdowney in Laois. (DOB 17/03/1930)

Kelly was convicted of two killings in London's Old Bailey in 1984. In July, as part of my research, I spoke to Nicky Meagher and Niall O'Doherty – both from Rathdowney – about remains they found on Kelly's old property, which is now Meagher's home, on the Ballybuggy Road in 1993.

O'Doherty was the local doctor then and Meagher now lives in a home built on the original Kelly site. Both men say Gardaí recovered the remains in 1993 but that they never heard anything since.

I have spoken on a number of occasions to Garda Eoin Everard in Portlaoise Garda Station. He has been following up. But I've heard nothing since August despite numerous contact attempts.

Can you tell me if the remains were recorded, forensically tested, and what the results were?

Please contact me if you need additional information.

Best regards

Garda Press Office
13/10/2016

Your email has been forwarded to the relevant section and we will revert in due course. It should be noted that all correspondence with An Garda Síochána should be through the Garda Press Office.

Brian Whelan Sergeant
Garda Press Office.

Chapter 36

Steadying the Ship

In the days that followed that email response from the Gardaí, I arranged to meet Ian Brown. Down a lane in the Kent countryside, his Mercedes was parked beside a quiet ditch on a winding road outside the town of Sevenoaks. It was silent, save for the tick-tick-tick of the engine as it cooled. In the driver's seat, Brown adjusted his large frame to get comfortable. He was a physically imposing man, with strong facial features, deep furrows and a thick head of hair. The leafy country setting felt somewhat at odds with the investigation's gritty stage sets around London, and a police career spent chasing criminals across the capital.

WHOOSHHHHHHH.

A car flew past on the lane stirring up a wave of air that sent the Mercedes into a gentle rock. Tick-tick-tick continued the engine as the lane fell quiet again. In the distance, the late afternoon sun was setting fast behind woodland turning a darker shade of green as the light faded below the tree line. Brown pressed his thumb on the button on his electronic cigarette and lifted the filter to his mouth. He took a drag. The device crackled and glowed. FFFFFFFFFFFFFffffffffff, he exhaled a cloud of vapour that escaped through a thin gap in the top of the driver's door window.

The former detective stared at a laptop balanced above the steering wheel in front of him. Between draws on his electronic cigarette, he carefully studied a version of Kelly's rap sheet that had been pieced together from conversations with the security source. Wary of the interview process as well as the media attention the story had attracted, Brown had been guarded and careful about what he revealed in the previous two meetings. He was also relying on the power of his recall and was somewhat hesitant on certain details but at the same time absolutely certain of his overall appraisal.

I explained about the archive at Kew and how the court files from the Boyd case had been withheld. I asked whether there was anything ongoing related to the current investigation that might be responsible. Something that someone didn't want revealed. Brown shook his head and appeared confused. 'I honestly don't know why the case files for the Boyd murder would have been withheld, or marked as being withheld. That doesn't make sense to me.' Now he was more comfortable, it was important for the former detective inspector to try and make sense of Kelly's confession. What cases did they have evidence for, but chose not to pursue? Just how many of Kelly's murder confessions *were* true?

'I remember a lot of these early crimes from Dublin,' said Brown, using his finger to pull the cursor down the screen. 'I remember getting Kelly's court files from Ireland. Ehhhhh, let me see' he muttered, and then began mumbling his way through some of the charges. 'Drunk. Assault. Assaulting a police officer, yeah, that was when he was sent to Broadmoor in 1969 after the aggravated robbery. But,' he continued, 'he wasn't there that long. Obviously, someone decided he was fit to be released. Shows you that we don't get it right all the time,' he said with a half-smile.

Brown had agreed to this meeting in an effort to get his story right. Two months earlier in Kent, he wouldn't be pushed to go on the public record about the Kelly case. But Platt's version of the story sowed the seed of deep annoyance and increasingly he felt he needed to put the record straight. 'I most probably wouldn't be talking about this now but for Platt,' he said, scrolling further through Kelly's timeline. 'I find it offensive for someone to claim what they did not do and *more* offensive when the person maligned is myself.

'I give lectures on cruise ships,' he said, widening the context. 'And I talk about the Kelly murder case. But it makes me look stupid when I stand on stage and talk about all these interviews in relation to Kelly and someone comes along and calls me a liar. I find that offensive and wrong.'

But if the story was so wrong, then why, I asked, has there been no public statement from the British Transport Police or the Met in an effort to reclaim the truth? 'Because it has been a tremendous waste of time trying to prove negatives in relation to some of Kelly's admissions,' he said. 'It is very difficult to prove something didn't happen and they have to look at all the allegations Platt made, and to the best of my knowledge, they have found nothing to substantiate *his* story.

'Platt's claims have taken months and months of work for *nothing*. And the last thing the police want is to open the whole thing up again – that's the last thing they need. I mean, I never even had a conversation with Geoff Platt. That's the crazy part. I got a phone call saying: "Have you seen the headlines? Have you seen this story about a mass murderer?"

'I thought, this is strange because I did those interviews with Kelly. That was the first feeling I had. Then I found so many things that did not add up about claims of what Geoff Platt did in the police and claims that were impossible to achieve in the timeframe of his career. I think Mr Platt got to the rank of uniformed sergeant. He was never a detective, as he said he was. And his claims of what he did in the police are mad. I think he did fifteen years and whatever it is about some of these claims, unfortunately, some people have believed them.

'It needs to be brought out that some of these claims are not true and some of them are ridiculous. He claimed to have been on the Krays' case and the Richardson crime family case but both [gangs] were on the opposite [side] of the water [the River Thames] and that would have been impossible. Many of these claims are fantasy.

'From memory, there were maybe ten interviews in all and Geoff Platt was never present,' he continued. 'The sergeant was Andy [Andre] Baker, who later became a commander and retired recently, and the detective chief superintendent was Ray Adams. He was the chief superintendent in charge of Brixton, Clapham and Kennington, and then the detective inspector was me.' The car fell silent. FFFFFFFFFFFFFFffffffffff went the electronic cigarette again.

Brown's assessment of Platt's testimony was withering, but at the same time his contemporary's often-fanciful account had reinvigorated a case that featured possible deaths never recorded. Not to mention victims whose lives had been deemed unworthy of the pursuit of justice. The former DI had himself claimed as much. And it was striking that the grievance now centred on ownership of the original investigation, rather than trying to decipher Kelly's death list.

Brown had been made aware of the fact Platt had worked on the Kelly case, but in his mind he must have been on the farthest reaches of the investigation. The former detective inspector just couldn't remember him. Maybe Platt *was* a small cog in the wheel of justice that turned Kelly's admissions into a conviction. But it was Ian Brown, Ray Adams, Andre Baker and others I'd been unable to track down – or who had been unwilling to talk – that had brought the case to its conclusion.

Using Officer A as a conduit, both Ray Adams and Andre Baker had declined to speak. Both were promoted in the years that followed the Kelly case, and Adams went on to become a police commander in south London, where he later found himself at the centre of corruption allegations following the landmark Stephen Lawrence murder case. And despite the disparity between the accounts of Platt and Brown, both former officers were absolutely certain of the same thing – Kelly was responsible for more than the deaths of two people. I asked Brown how many murders he could say with certainty that Kelly *was* responsible for.

'I think the hours and hours we spent with him and his bravado and his willingness to talk about all he'd done – except Toal, the one he was found not guilty of – that in the end, Kelly put his hands up to maybe thirteen, fourteen, fifteen murders and we proved maybe five or six,' he said.

'Boyd.

'Fisher.

'Toal in Kennington – he definitely did that one that he was acquitted for.

'Scotch Jack who he hit on the head with a brick.

'The poisoning of Mick Dunne in Tooting.

'He ended up being in prison during one of them in Coronation Buildings, but was he a serial killer? Yes, he strangled and stabbed and killed tramps. It was very unusual to discover a tramp murdered in the cell first of all and then that discovery turns into a serial killer and someone who confesses to it, and is proud of it.'

Whether Kelly was proud of his crimes and derived satisfaction from committing the murders for which he was convicted is not known, but Brown remembers criminal psychologists poring over the killer's profile. For the former DI, this only complicated Kelly. It always felt like a self-serving effort to find some explanation from his childhood that could be presented to civilized society.

'Killers are usually a deranged person who has a fetish for one thing, but Kelly was just a tramp murderer,' he said. 'He didn't go into Kennington Park the night Edward Toal was murdered looking for someone to kill – it just happened. He would get drunk and violent and he knew no bounds as to where that violence was going to take him. He was a violent drunk, a tramp who was prepared to murder. He hated tramps, he was one; he hated alcoholics, he was one; he hated homosexuals, and I believe that was the reason he killed Fisher.

'I didn't even know a Mr Fisher had been murdered. That was six years before I went to Clapham and Kelly was one of the tramps who was interviewed for it originally. But where it was strange is that I ask one question about the murder he was acquitted of, Edward Toal, and he'd never admit to that murder. The reason was, he was found not guilty by the judge and so as far as he was concerned he'd not done that one. But then he confessed to one we knew nothing about and that was a watershed moment and he told us, because he wanted to show he was more clever – that it was a robbery and he was too clever for us.'

By now, darkness had descended and lights speckled from the hillside in the distance. I considered what Brown was saying. His certainty over the crimes Kelly was convicted of and the ones they could have returned further convictions for was something he articulated with great confidence. I asked him how he felt about John Slater's position – that Kelly should be judged on the convictions listed on the laptop in front of him, not admissions that never received due process.

'Hmmmmm', he said with a frown. 'Well, if someone confesses to a crime, freely and willingly, then you accept their word and he should be judged on what he was – a tramp murderer with a violent temper. If he broke on a bender he became violent and he'd no compunction about what he would do. I have no doubt Kelly did everything he told us. Because if someone confesses to two murders, he's found guilty of them and then he also confesses to murdering others, then as a detective you have good grounds to believe that he did what he said – only none of them were on the underground.'

I asked Brown if it needed to be solidified with more than an admission. 'We put Kelly down as a serial killer upon his say-so and all the murders he put up as having done were investigated,' explained Brown. 'His admissions are only factual if you can find things in that murder that only the killer could have known, and we did in some of them. And after we confirmed five or six, then it was logical to assume that the others he'd confessed to are right.

'In the case of Scotch Jack, who was found at the bottom of a basement stairs with a blunt trauma injury to the head – this happened. And detectives discovered that a man did stagger into the casualty ward of a Tooting hospital and die of acute alcohol poisoning. There was also an arson case where Kelly set fire to a building and the tramps there could finger him as being present in the building that night.

'Like I said, he stood and told us that he'd done thirteen, fourteen, maybe fifteen murders. It's my professional opinion – and no one is completely right, but we had evidence – that Kelly did five, maybe six, no more than that. At the time of his conviction he was one of the most prolific murderers in British history and he was later overtaken by Harold Shipman. And there's not much more to say, other than the claims of thirty-one murders is a piece of Geoff Platt fantasy.'

Chapter 37

Light at the End of the Tunnel?

In this story of murder and cover-up, one essential voice was missing in terms of determining – as close as possible – what was fantasy and what was truth in the Kieran Kelly case. Just how far did the pendulum swing back towards Ian Brown's 'five or six' murders from the figure of thirty-one being peddled by the former policeman Platt? Or was it in fact just two killings as flagged up by John Slater?

So far, official voices had been notably absent, from the Home Office to the Met, to the London Underground, the British Transport Police and the UK Prison Service. And Platt's story screamed into the void this created. Officer A had confirmed that a review of the Kelly files had taken place and that the original investigation team, as well as Slater, had been contacted after the Met's top policeman committed to looking into the case during an interview on the BBC.

Eventually, the British Transport Police agreed to a meeting at their offices in Camden, north London. Detective Superintendent Gary Richardson had access to the case files. He was at the back end of a long career and not unlike Brown and Platt in terms of physical appearance – tall and imposing, a throwback maybe to a period of recruitment when physique and stature were an important factor.

In his second-floor office, Richardson was seated behind his desk, dressed in a crisp white shirt and a neatly fitting tie that ran long below his navel. We had planned to head to a cafe but it was raining. 'Looks like we'll have to cancel that coffee,' he said, turning in his chair and looking out the window. Then he hollered out the office door for someone to bring in two cups of coffee.

Files as thick as telephone books were stacked up on the desk in front of him, with covers faded to an orangey-brown. Inside, separate files were bundled into sections divided by crumpled coloured tabs. Detective Superintendent (DS) Richardson started leafing through the pages. It was his responsibility to assist the Met in review of the Kelly case files, though it was a duty he'd been dragged away from in recent months because of an accident involving a tram in Croydon that left seven people dead.

'So you've spoken to Mr Platt then,' he asked while opening one of the folders. '*Look*, here,' he said fiddling a piece of paper free from a file. 'There's a commendation,' he announced, holding up the page for inspection. 'Ian Brown, Ray Adams, Geoff Platt and DCI Clabby,' he read aloud, confirming the names of those who'd been granted a commendation in the case.

'There is no doubt Geoff Platt worked on the case,' he continued before I could even ask the question. 'That he could have brought Kelly to and from the courts. That's what went on then. We didn't have security companies to do it like we do now. And he probably handled evidence. Some of Kelly's interviews were recorded on an old Nagra machine. It's possible Geoff Platt *could* have been in the room during one of the interviews – but no, he wasn't asking the questions.'

Richardson continued leafing through the files and explained that he'd interviewed Platt about his version of the Kelly story, *and* Ian Brown. Platt had even signed a copy of his book on Kelly and posted it to him and his investigation team.

'Here,' he declared after a short pause. 'Yes, look – here you have Kelly admitting to four murders after he murdered Boyd in the cell. But he says two of that four *could* have sustained injuries that they *might* have died from.'

Richardson continued flicking through the file, plucking information at random. It was a disorderly presentation, but reflected his objective to highlight a case where confusion and contradiction reigned at every turn and on every page. 'Look,' he announced theatrically again. 'Here is his original arrest sheet, where Kelly robbed a ring off an old man, Walter Bell.' He paused and started to read the original text. 'Kelly sat down beside the man. There was some kind of exchange and then he claimed Kelly made a homosexual advance. Blah, blah, blah.

'Then, Kelly wrestled the man's arm around his back and removed the ring from his little finger. He then went and sat down on a bench beside another man. Bell came back across looking for the ring back. It was worth roughly £25,' said Richardson, glancing up and then down at the file notes again. 'And the men got into an argument until the police arrived and arrested Kelly. And it all started from there,' he said, closing the file.

Listening to Richardson's random extractions from Kelly's case notes raised yet again the issue of his sexuality, which loomed large over the case. And I thought *again* about the suggestion that the killer's crimes were in some way motivated by a deviant sexual undercurrent. Platt said Kelly told him that he was a homosexual. Brown said that some of Kelly's crimes were driven by the suppression of his homosexuality. Yet his former employer, builder Brian Sliman, said that in the four years he knew him there was absolutely no indication that Kieran Kelly was gay.

'Is there anything in Kelly's statements where he says he was gay?' I asked. 'No, I don't think so,' said Richardson. 'Not according to his own words.' Kelly's sexuality had been identified as a major factor in his motivation to kill, not only by the media, but by the officer in charge of the case. I had wondered whether the killer would have made any official reference to this in a statement, or more than one statement, and that it would have been written large in his file. It could also have been the case that an embarrassed Kelly never included this fact in an official statement, or that the scrutiny of related documents by DS Richardson had been less than thorough.

At the same time, two former police officers, independent of each other, had flagged up his sexuality as a big motivator to kill. 'We sent experienced interviewers out to meet Geoff Platt and they came back exasperated, saying they couldn't pin him down. There's just no substance to a lot of what he is saying,' said Richardson. 'I remember the first time I ever spoke to him, he told me he was ex-CID in Brixton and that he ran the team there. Then I started asking him years and dates and he'd be jumping all over the place.

'Roughly one person a day throws themselves on to a train line here. After Geoff brought out his version of events people did get in touch. I can't remember how many exactly, but people saying that there was an aunt or an uncle that committed suicide. And some contacted Geoff Platt directly. But it was clutching at straws really.

'The thing is the cases were investigated thoroughly at the time. If they were investigating Kelly's claims of a murder in Bournemouth – a stabbing – and no body turned up, then that was what was done at the time. When we are building a case, we identify all the crimes associated with the person and then who is saying what. What's the source? Who's providing this information? Then we take it from there.'

Richardson returned to the file. I explained that I'd been directed to a document by Officer A, that appeared to summarize the cases and confessions Kelly made to police – beyond the two killings he was convicted for. I produced the document and handed it to the DS who studied the appendix of murders Kelly had committed, attempted murders he was acquitted of, cases that never made it to court, and murder claims that had proved impossible to verify.

There were thirteen entries and at the end of each one an outcome was listed. In the numbers game that was the Kieran Kelly story, this single piece of paper represented a total of the police efforts, more than twelve months after Platt projected the case into the public consciousness. It was a list of conclusions, many closed, and minus the kind of speculation that both marked the case out and elevated it. In a slow deliberate movement, Detective Superintendent Gary Richardson handed the document across the table.

APPENDIX

Offence: Murder

Date: 1953
Source: *Daily Star*/Boyd Interviews
Victim: Christy Smith
Location: Baker Street/Stockwell Tube
Summary: Kelly states he pushed him under a train.
Investigation: Extensive enquiries have failed to trace any record of such incident.

Offence: Murder

Date: 1973
Source: Boyd interviews
Victim: Bearded Man
Location: Vauxhall
Summary: Kelly states he hit the male over the head with a bit of a bar and buried him in a building opposite the Tate Library. This building was pulled down and body not discovered.

Investigation: Enquiries can again find no incident but it is a fact that the houses referred to were demolished about 1978. It is felt this matter can be taken no further because there is neither a body nor corroboration.

Offence: Stabbing

Date: 1973
Victim: Unknown male
Location: Bournemouth
Source: Boyd interviews
Summary: Kelly states he stabbed the man with a knife.
Investigation: Enquiries can find no trace of a vagrant or any other person dying from knife wounds in Bournemouth area and there is [sic] no outstanding murder enquiries of this nature.

Offence: Murder

Date: 1973
Victim: Unknown male
Location: Shepherd's Bush
Source: Boyd interviews
Summary: Kelly states he kicked him in the head.
Investigation: Enquiries can reveal no trace of an incident relating to the facts given by Kelly.

Offence: Murder

Date: July 1975
Victim: Hector John Fisher
Location: Clapham Common
Source: Boyd interviews
Summary: Kelly admitted that he hit Fisher across the head with a metal bar/heavy knife and then stabbed Fisher a number of times.
Investigation: Charged with murder and trial held at same time as Boyd trial. Found guilty and given a life sentence.

Offence: Murder

Date: 15/04/1976
Victim: Unknown male
Location: Coronation Buildings
Source: Boyd Interviews
Summary: Kelly states he went to a flat owned by Paddy Kelly, a regular drinking haunt for vagrants. Kelly forced drink down a drunken sleeping man until he started to vomit. Kelly states that the Coroner brought a verdict that the man had choked on his own vomit.
Investigation: Enquiries reveal that an incident, almost identical in every way, happened on the 15/04/1976. A check on Kelly's criminal record and further enquiries with Wandsworth Prison reveal that Kelly, on this date, was serving a term of two years' imprisonment and can be safely assumed that Kelly did not leave the confines of Wandsworth Prison. Vagrants at the scene were traced and who state Kelly wasn't present.

Offence: Murder

Date: 31/05/1977
Victim: Edward Toal
Location: Kennington Park
Source: Edward Toal interviews
Summary: Kelly admits that he strangled Toal.
Investigation: Kelly was acquitted for murder and manslaughter.

Offence: Murder

Date: 02/06/1977
Victim: Maurice Weighly
Location: Soho
Source: *Daily Star Sunday* Newspaper
Summary: Maurice Weighly was found dead in Soho, his face and genitals had been mutilated. The neck of a broken bottle had been thrust up his rectum. Police found Kelly and another tramp in the neighbourhood with blood stains on their clothing.

Investigation: Kelly was charged with murder, his companion described the crime in grisly detail. Six months passed before the trial and Kelly was acquitted after the State's key witness [was] an alcoholic 'blind drunk' at the time of the murder. The witness subsequently vanished and was never seen again. Kelly later admitted to this murder in 1983.

Offence: Attempted Murder

Date: 31/08/1982
Victim: Francis Taylor
Location: Tooting Bec Tube
Source: *Daily Star*/PNC
Summary: Pushed male under tube.
Investigation: Not guilty verdict returned by jury.

Offence: Murder

Date: 23/08/1982
Victim: Micky Dunne
Location: Tooting
Source: Boyd interviews
Summary: Kelly states that he was responsible for the death of Mick Dunne who he mixed a drink of surgical spirit, orange and pills for and sat in a park and watched him drink it and gave Dunne a beating. Dunne was taken away and found dead in King's College hospital of Cirrhosis of the liver.
Investigation: Enquiries reveal that another vagrant, O'Connor, was drinking with Kelly and Dunne near the library at Tooting Broadway. O'Connor left to purchase more cider and on his return he found that Kelly and Dunne had been fighting and on his return, Kelly left with two males. The following day Dunne was unable to walk and had badly swollen legs. Dunne and O'Connor went to Camberwell medical centre. Dunne recovered and then took a turn for the worse starting on the 28/08/82. Pathologist examined Dunne and found that he had died from bronchopneumonia and

cryogenic cirrhosis of the liver. Submission put forward to charge Kelly with murder.

Offence: Attempted Murder

Date: 1983
Victim: Unknown male
Location: Kennington Tube
Source: *Daily Star*
Summary: Pushed male onto rails but driver stopped in time.
Investigation: N/A

Offence: Attempted murder

Date: 1983
Victim: Jock Gordon/Gordon McMurray
Location: Oval
Source: *Daily Star*
Summary: Pushed male onto rails but male rescued by off-duty Tube worker.
Investigation: Kelly told his solicitor he pushed Jock Gordon onto the railway lines at Oval, enquiries with John O'Connor identified Gordon as Gordon McMurray. McMurray was located and he stated that he could identify the person who pushed him. An ID parade was performed and McMurray positively identified Kelly. This incident was not reported and enquiries to trace the employee who helped him proved negative. Submissions put forward to charge Kelly with attempted murder.

Offence: Murder

Date: 04/08/1983
Victim: William Boyd
Location: Clapham Police Station
Source: Boyd interviews
Summary: Strangled and beat the male to death in the prison cells.

Investigation: Found guilty of this offence as well as Fisher and
admitted to other offences.

The police investigations into the Kelly case listed the
manslaughter conviction for Boyd and the murder conviction
for Fisher. It included five cases without any trace of evidence
in relation to Christy Smith at Baker Street, the stabbing in
Bournemouth, the beating in Shepherd's Bush, the bricking
in Vauxhall, and the mutilation of a man named as Maurice
Weighly in Soho – a charge that had been raised by Platt.

There was the garroting acquittal for Edward Toal, the
acquittal of attempted murder against Francis Taylor, a
submission had been made to charge Kelly with murder of
Mickey Dunne who'd been poisoned in Tooting, and two
other incidents at Kennington and Oval Underground stations
of men being pushed in front of tube trains. But only one could
be identified – Gordon McMurray, who survived.

The crime appendix backed up much of what Brown
had been saying with the exception of the claim of murder
against a man called Scotch Jack in Vauxhall in 1973.
Meanwhile, the details undermined and corroborated
some of Platt's account. But how much confidence could
be applied to the document? It was impossible to know
how much the police had invested in their review of each of
these entries. With the perpetrator dead, many of the key
witnesses deceased and a case file that was error-strewn
and littered with conflicting information, the quest to find
out how many people Kelly murdered was always destined
to leave loose ends.

I suspected that now, like then, the resources thrown at
the case would have been limited. Against the backdrop of
swingeing police budget cuts, a cold-case investigation into
claims of murder dating back to the 1950s was going to be
some distance down the list of police priorities. Reading the
list of entries and outcomes, Richardson said the Met had

shouldered the burden of the investigation and that: 'they (the original investigators) had done all they could.'

Outside the window of Gary Richardson's second-floor office, it was still raining. 'You know,' said the DS, breaking the silence that had been granted to study the crime appendix. 'Kelly is someone who murdered a person in the cells.' He flipped the file closed and leaned back into his chair. 'Anyone who is capable of that, is capable of doing a lot of these crimes.'

Chapter 38

End of the Line

It had been more than four months since I'd met Geoff Platt in Stoke, and the piecing together of the Kelly story demanded the deconstruction of his account. After all, it was Platt's testimony that set in motion a chain of events that led to a police review of the case. But despite the meeting with Detective Superintendent Richardson in Camden, it felt like the Kelly case had yet to be marked with the full stop his crime appendix had provided. And Platt's version continued to loom large. The former policeman had appeared as if from nowhere with a story of crime and cover-up only to then disappear just as fast, before emerging again with equal vigour.

I had discovered through Officer A that there was a surprising reason behind his temporary retreat from the public eye. It was because Platt was not only an ex-policeman, but also an ex-prisoner. And he'd been locked up for a period not long after he'd brought the Kelly story into the public arena. This had nothing to do with his resurrection of the murder case. According to Officer A, Platt was sent to jail after driving his car on the wrong side of the road towards a group of children after growing impatient at a pedestrian crossing. That reckless rush of blood to the head that had allegedly saved a fellow officer from an axeman had, in the civilian world, left a young girl injured and traumatized after being clipped by Platt's Land Rover.

A news story detailing the November 2013 incident had been published in the *Daily Mail*, and cited claims by the former officer that he'd guarded royalty, as well as former prime ministers John Major and Margaret Thatcher. There was other reportage related to Platt online. Prior to the emergence of the Kelly story, the former policeman was the feature of two long-form articles in both *The Times* and Stoke's local newspaper, *The Sentinel*. They detailed a stellar police career and his work with disadvantaged young males. There was another, in a local paper in Croydon. This time, involving an altercation between the former policeman and a member of the public that had left Platt in fear of his life.

Then, in 2015, the headlines changed. Now the column inches and airtime were dedicated to his role in resurrecting the Kelly story through the claims in his book. Claims of a cover-up of a secret serial killer that were taken so seriously by Scotland Yard, that it forced a police investigation. It had compelled one of the lead investigating officers, Detective Inspector Ian Brown, to go on public record about it for the first time in over thirty years in an attempt to clarify the truth and defend the work he'd put into closing a traumatic case.

But while the modest Brown had reluctantly stepped into the spotlight, it was obvious that being in the public gaze wasn't an uncomfortable experience for Platt. From news coverage in the print media, to interviews on the BBC and RTÉ in Ireland, the ex-policeman appeared to relish the attention. And by late summer 2016, he appeared to be missing it.

By then, the Kelly story had moved to Ireland and beyond his reach. The search for the truth had opened up new fronts in Kelly's hometown and widened to include new voices. This new narrative had rendered the voice of the former policeman temporarily redundant. However, in the dying days of summer, he'd sent me a sensational text message wherein he disclosed that Kelly wasn't the only Irish killer he'd arrested. There were others. And he was happy to meet to discuss them, too!

I felt certain that this text message was a punt to remain relevant. I knew that Platt had been playing fast and loose with the facts. Recordings made in the North Stafford Hotel detailed how the British Transport Police had called him to a meeting in their offices in Camden, where Platt claimed there was a stack of Kelly case files embossed with his signature – prison release dockets, witness statements, court files. Much of the legwork in the Kelly case was down to him, he said. Sourcing files, helping prepare interviews, collecting Kelly from prison and bringing him to be interviewed. For this he'd received the commendation contained in DS Richardson's file.

'I spoke to the police and they said they like everything,' he had said on the recordings. 'But they don't like the thirty-one murders. And the only other thing they said they couldn't believe was that I was responsible for conducting the inquiry. I'm not saying I was the brains, I'm saying I was the legs. I never claimed to be the investigating officer. But I did do the legwork.

'After the first two weeks I did all the legwork. Two weeks after Boyd, they all returned to office duties and I was the only one who stayed on the inquiry. They said: "We've now seen the case papers and your name is the only name on there, other than Detective Ian Brown", and that the original investigation team were under supervision from two CID commanders in Scotland Yard who were applying pressure to play down deaths.'

After bringing the Kelly story into the public domain, the natural conclusion to the investigation demanded one final meeting with Platt. How would he explain the opposing narratives of former Detective Inspector Ian Brown, Officer A, Detective Superintendent Gary Richardson, solicitor John Slater and Kelly's former employer Brian Sliman? And what of the members of the public who had approached the police, believing their family members had died at the hands of Kelly, and not by suicide, on the Northern Line?

Platt claimed to be in possession of original police recordings that could grant him the kind of credibility that could buttress his testimony. So, I called and asked to meet. I wanted him to bring the audio recordings of Kelly's admissions; to address errors he'd made with dates and years; to try and match, or strike out, those parts of his testimony that corroborated with what Brown was saying, or further contradicted it; to give him the benefit of the doubt regarding parts of his testimony.

Upon answering the phone, the first thing Platt wanted to know was whether the Irish police had come back with anything on 'the body in the garden in Ireland' before excitedly explaining that he'd further evidence on the Kelly case, explosive evidence that was going to cause the Home Office and the police even more discomfort. We decided to meet in Clapham Common and walk through the murder scene at the back of Holy Trinity church, where the body of Hector Fisher was found in 1975. Platt agreed to travel by train from Stoke.

* * *

It was a cold but bright Friday morning in October. I arrived early and waited in the window seat of a Starbucks coffee shop directly opposite the entrance to Clapham Common tube station for Geoff Platt to arrive. The decision to meet on Clapham Common was in part driven by the need to meet in a public place. I was planning on interrogating Platt's often surreal account. I wanted to be on terrain I knew and in a setting that felt comfortable.

People flashed by on roller blades. Others idled past on bicycles. Women joggers wearing Lycra pushed prams, walkers cast out dogs attached to long leads and commuters hurried down the entrance to the station carrying coffees and copies of the free morning newspaper, the *Metro*.

This vibrant morning setting on Clapham Common was at odds with the dark, forbidding place once frequented by Kieran Kelly, but some of the furniture of that subterranean world remained. The common's mature trees had grown a thicker branch and just a couple of hundred yards away from the station entrance, the steeple of Holy Trinity church reached high above the foliage. It was behind this church that the stabbed and badly beaten body of Hector Fisher was discovered slumped on a bench in July 1975.

Suddenly Platt appeared out of the station entrance carrying a small sports bag, dressed in a pair of loose-fitting pale-coloured jeans and a zip-up fleece, half closed. He stopped, as if uncertain and anxiously looked up and down the street. When we met he explained that he'd packed and carefully folded an ironed shirt and tie that he would change into for the purpose of taking some photographs after the interview. The shirt was visible through the partially opened zip of his sports bag, but there was no mention of the case notes or the audio recordings he'd said he would bring. Was this going to be another example of all style and no substance?

'This used to be my beat around here,' said Platt, as we set off down the gentle slope towards Holy Trinity church. 'Years ago, when I was working plain clothes.' I pointed out that other police sources had described him as a plain-clothes police officer rather than the image of detective he'd presented to the media. He grumbled and we continued on towards the church, the sound of the traffic fading as we sank deeper into the common. At the entrance, a gate opened from a small fence into the grounds. Entering the church, Platt waved in no particular direction. 'He was found there,' he said. 'Fisher, yes,' he continued, offering no closer fix on the exact location.

We stood in the sun and started the recorded interview. A couple of hundred yards away, cars skirted the common's green perimeter, their engines now barely audible. Platt placed his bag at his feet and zipped up his fleece and I began by asking him if it was possible to talk with certainty only about the murders of William Boyd and Hector Fisher. 'The director of prosecutions said the evidence was there for twenty-four murders,' he replied. 'And on this bench – this is where Kelly was accused of murdering Fisher.'

I asked him where he was when Fisher was murdered in 1975. 'I had just joined the Met and was not involved in that investigation at all,' he replied. 'A big squad was set up. They spoke to all the witnesses; there were dozens. It was all filed and it was not until after '83, and Boyd, that Kelly raised the murder.'

'John Slater said Fisher wasn't stabbed in the bollocks,' I pointed out. 'There was a police investigation and this isn't a matter of dispute.'

'Kelly said he attacked him around the privates,' Geoff replied. 'He thought he was a queer who dressed in women's clothes and there were injuries around the privates but I am not sure whether it was a direct stabbing.'

'In the last weeks I've spoken to Ian Brown and John Slater,' I continued. 'And there is a lot of variance in what you have to say and what they have to say. They both said you contacted neither of them and then you write a book about it, but you don't get closer to the case than them.'

'I've contacted John Slater on dozens of occasions,' said Platt. 'I met John Slater for lunch in Clapham Junction to talk about it and asked to meet again and meet him regularly and I had no way to speak to Ian Brown, but then I've seen the case papers in a way he hasn't.'

'The police say they have their own recordings and you have yours?' I queried.

'Yes!' confirmed Geoff.

'From where?'

'From the police station.'

'But they say you were not in the room. That it was Ian Brown, Andre Baker and Ray Adams and you received a commendation, but you came in later.'

'I wasn't present in the room, I'll grant you,' said Platt. 'But I spent more time than they did chasing up the facts, and officers said I had an exceptional memory and there was no issue there.'

He paused. 'There was no need to speak to everyone,' he said thoughtfully.

'But you are an ex-police detective,' I appealed. 'It would be expected that you would have talked to the lead detective. You said a number of times that you were the only person alive that knew Kelly, but Ian Brown knew him and John Slater knew him and they are both alive.'

'OK, I'll give you that,' replied Geoff. 'But John Slater's involvement isn't as deep, but there you go – I'm happy,' he said defiantly.

'People are uncomfortable because the public would expect the kind of rigour from an ex-police officer that has been absent here,' I said. 'They would have expected extensive conversations.'

At that moment Platt removed his hand from his pocket, leaned down and lifted up his bag. 'OK, well, I'm sorry to have troubled you,' he said and then turned on his heels and took off across the common towards the road. I followed, asking him if the interview was over. He ignored the question and continued walking, ever further away from the church, his footsteps rustling through a carpet of brown leaves, his eyes fixed on the road ahead.

'We're finished,' he muttered, before checking his step and turning to walk back up the slope in the direction of the tube station.

'We're finished? Why?' I asked.

'I've had enough,' he said breaking into a more purposeful stride.

'This will reflect badly,' I said. 'You still have the chance to take ownership of the story. There are people who lost loved ones on the Northern Line and it's only fair to ask questions on behalf of those people who *can't* ask them.'

He continued to ignore the questions and by now we were within 50 yards of the entrance to Clapham Common Underground Station.

'GEOFF!'

No reply.

'GEOFF!'

He disappeared down the stairs into the underground, without so much as a backwards glance, lost among the commuters.

Standing outside the station and on the edge of the common, early afternoon traffic streamed by and warm air from the bowels of the station flowed up the stairwell. It was possible to hear the screeching sound of steel train wheels arriving and departing from the station, deep below. And Geoff Platt was gone, swallowed by the same transport network he portrayed as Kelly's killing ground.

Epilogue

July 2018, nearly two years after Geoff Platt fled the scene of the interview on Clapham Common, Ian Brown was sitting in a small cafe in Penge High Street in south-east London. It was mid-morning, R&B played over the cafe's sound system and the former detective took a sip of tea from a heavy white mug. Then he gently pushed his phone across the table with the finger of his free hand. 'Have a look at that,' he said, nodding at the screen and taking a bite from his sandwich. 'He's doing talks on cruise ships now. Look at his biography down the side,' he pointed. 'He's made himself a doctor. *Doctor* Geoff Platt.'

In the months that followed that final meeting with Platt, the British Transport Police disclosed that they weren't going to commit any further resources to the Kelly case. They'd brought the investigation as far as they could and DS Gary Richardson had politely declined to engage with any further questions related to the case. Beyond the appendix of Kelly's crimes and admissions – and the summary sheet that had been handed over in his office in Camden – there was nothing further he could add.

But while Platt disappeared into the underground that October morning, he continued to advance *his* Kieran

Kelly story, which received another notable spike in press coverage on New Year's Eve 2016, three months after the confrontation on the common. In a *Daily Mail* report, Platt even detailed the discovery of skeletal remains on the site of Kelly's former home in Ireland and again listed Kelly's body count as thirty-one.

I brought the article to Brown's attention as we sat in the cafe in Penge. 'So many of these claims are outrageous,' said the former detective, clearly affronted. 'They are a slight on me and the allegation that the Met and the Home Office conspired to stop murders being investigated on the underground because it would terrify London commuters is a load of rubbish. Sensationalism at its worst.

'This has caused all sorts of trouble,' he continued. 'And what gets me is that no one in the media bothered to check whether Geoff Platt's version of events was true or not. There were no background checks and no calls to insiders to see if all these claims were true. Everyone just ran with the story and the truth has been trying to catch up ever since. I give lectures on crime and the Kelly case is one of them and Geoff Platt is still putting out information that many people are accepting as the truth.

'I understand now, that he was an aide to CID, an apprentice PC out of uniform. He never made detective and left that inquiry after all the Kelly interviews. Kelly was brought up to Lambeth Magistrates' Court for his remand hearings and Platt was employed to run Kelly from Brixton Prison to all his court appearances. There is no doubt he would have talked to Kelly a lot and he got a commendation on that case for his work with Kelly after his arraignment. But he had no connection to the investigation. I told the same thing to Gary Richardson when I went to meet him.' Brown lifted the heavy white mug to his mouth and took another sip from his tea.

'What have the police in Ireland come back with in relation to testing the bones?' he asked after resting the mug back down on the table. I explained that despite persistent phone calls and emails over a period of more than a year, the Gardaí had continually declined to give any explanation whatsoever on the discovery. It was like they didn't have one.

It seemed the house call to Nicky Meagher's property in Rathdowney in 1993 had gone unrecorded for whatever reason. Possibly, at the time, it felt like too much work, or work thought not to be necessary. Ironically, Kelly was still alive in 1993 and incarcerated in prison. Had the Gardaí notified their counterparts in England, then there would have been an opportunity to question him about the discovery. That never happened. Possibly, it never would have happened even if they had.

Kelly's victims were homeless, troubled souls who lived on the margins of society. By Ian Brown's admission, a lack of resources and, sadly, interest had meant more recent victims on English soil had not received justice as pursuing the cases would not have affected Kelly's sentence. So the discovery of what may have been human remains, in Ireland, would not have been welcomed in a case that lacked thoroughness and rigour in terms of following up Kelly's admission.

The profile of credible witnesses in Nicky Meagher and Niall O'Doherty may have also challenged an investigation that had in previous times relied on struggling addicts. Only there was no recorded discovery of any skeleton with a wire noose around its neck. Just like there were no bodies to back up many of Kelly's admissions.

I brought Brown's attention to the crime appendix that listed the outcomes of Kelly's murders and claims of murder. And one case in particular, the alleged murder of Maurice Weighly in Soho in 1977. Weighly was another homeless victim whose badly mutilated body was said to be found in a Soho alleyway. The *Daily Star Sunday* was the attributed source according to the police record. But this case never registered with Ian Brown. 'I can't say I remember that one or remember that being part of any investigation,' he said with a shrug.

The former DI was more interested in finding out more about the discovery of physical evidence in Ireland and the outcome of that discovery. 'It's just speculation now of course,' he said, sipping his tea. 'But that was Kelly's style wasn't it? Around the neck – the wire noose I mean. You had the one in the park, Edward Toal, where he took the rope off his trousers and pulled it around his neck. Then in the cell with Boyd, he tied his socks around his neck too. Attacking the neck, that *was* his signature move.'

But like the claim of return visits of Kelly's mother to the site of this burial in Rathdowney, how her son spent the final years of his life remained a big unknown. I relayed to Brown how, since out last meeting, I'd contacted Frankland Prison in Durham, where according to official records, Kieran Kelly had seen out his final days. Or had he?

In recent months, I'd requested Kelly's death certificate and upon receipt I realized the certificate contained information that made the police record of Kelly's death feel less than certain. The certificate revealed that Kieran Patrick Kelly had died of respiratory illness in 2001. He was aged 71. Only his location of death was not given as the prison, but a house on a residential road.

Number 55 Finchale Avenue was a detached, two-storey home in an area of Durham called Brasside, close to the prison. The redbrick home was now possessed of a paved driveway and a stand-alone garage. Officer A had been unable to offer any definitive explanation as to why the location of death of a man sentenced to spend the rest of his days behind Frankland's curtain wall, was a pleasant-looking home with a view of green fields.

Quite possibly, the building belonged to the prison and the institution used a residential address for the purpose of marking the deaths of deceased inmates. But in the same way that the prison services declined to allow a visit to the prison, or facilitate any meeting to ascertain more information on Kelly's incarceration, they too had been unwilling to offer any clarification on why the location of death wasn't the prison itself.

Sitting in the cafe, the irony of this development wasn't lost on the conversation. Not only was it impossible to prove the location of death for some of Kelly's victims, but so too, the killer himself. 'Like I said before, we had him for five or six murders,' shrugged Brown lifting the mug to his mouth and taking another sip. 'This sounds like just another thing about the Kelly case that we'll probably never know.'

Timeline

Kieran Kelly's Significant Dates

1930
Kieran Patrick Kelly, born 17 March.

1942
Confirmation ceremony in St Kevin's Catholic Church, Harrington Street, Dublin.

1953
Kelly claimed he murdered his friend Christy Smith at Baker Street Underground Station, London. He also appeared in Dublin District Court and is sentenced to two years' probation for stealing.

1957
Dublin, sentenced to two years' hard labour for stealing, shop breaking and house breaking.

1960
Moved to London.

1961
Married in Church of the Sacred Heart, Camberwell, Southwark, to Frances Esther Territt.

1965
Convicted of assaulting a police officer.

1969
Sent to Broadmoor Hospital following a robbery that involved an aggravated assault.

1973
Claimed to have stabbed a man to death in Bournemouth, beaten a man – Scotch Jack – to death with an iron bar in Vauxhall and kicked an unnamed homeless man to death in Shepherd's Bush.

1975
Interviewed and then released following the murder of Hector Fisher on Clapham Common.

1976
Unidentified male died after choking to death on his own vomit in Coronation Buildings, Vauxhall.

1977
The year identified by the *Daily Star Sunday* newspaper related to the alleged murder confession of a Maurice Weighly.

1977
Edward Toal found strangled to death in Kennington Park.

1982
Francis Taylor pushed onto the train line at Tooting Bec Underground Station on the Northern Line. Mickey Dunne poisoned with a cocktail of surgical spirits in Tooting.

1983
Gordon McMurray, aka Jock Gordon, pushed onto the tracks at Oval Underground Station. William Boyd found strangled to death in Clapham Police Station. Kelly confessed to the murder of Hector Fisher and many others.

1984
Kieran Kelly is tried and convicted at the Old Bailey for the manslaughter of William Boyd and the murder of Hector Fisher.

1985
Kelly denied and appealed the charge of murder against Hector Fisher.

1993
Nicky Meagher found skeletal remains on the site of Kieran Kelly's former home in Rathdowney, County Laois, Ireland.

2001
Kieran Kelly died in Frankland Prison, Durham.

2015
Geoff Platt authored *The London Underground Serial Killer*. The Met chief of police, Sir Bernard Hogan-Howe, committed to a reappraisal of the Kelly story.

The Times, September 1983

Man accused of murder faces new death charge
Kieran Patrick Kelly who is accused of killing a vagrant in a police station cell, faced another murder charge when he appeared at South Weston Magistrates Court in Battersea, south London yesterday.

Mr Kelly, aged 53, unemployed and of no fixed address, was accused of murdering Mr Hector Fisher in July 1975. Mr Fisher, a bachelor, who lived in a flat in Wandsworth Road, Clapham, south London, was found with head injuries in a churchyard at Clapham Common.

Mr Kelly is also charged with murdering Mr William Boyd, aged 53, at Clapham Police Station on August 4, and robbing Mr Walter Bell of a ring worth £25 in Clapham on the same date.

Mr Francis Jones for Mr Kelly made no application for bail. He was remanded in custody until September 30.

The Huffington Post, July 2015

London Underground Serial Killer Kiernan Kelly 'Murdered 16 People By Pushing Them Onto Tube Tracks'

A former Scotland Yard detective has alleged police deliberately 'hushed up' the murders of 16 people by a serial killer who claimed to have pushed victims to their deaths on the London Underground during the 1970s.

Geoff Platt says Irish drifter Kiernan Kelly confessed to the killings when he questioned him over the murder of his prison cellmate William Boyd in 1984. Kelly had been picked up that year for being drunk and disorderly.

Platt, 60, recalls interrogating Kelly in his new book *The London Underground Serial Killer.*

Platt told the *Daily Star*: 'He was high – high on adrenaline, testosterone…aroused. You could see it in his eyes. He was proud of that murder and when we went to speak to him he just confessed to killing 16 other people.'

Platt says his first instincts were that Kelly was a fantasist but that further investigations revealed he had indeed been at the scene of a number of reported suicides on the Tube.

He told *The Huffington Post UK* that Kelly revealed his first victim was his own best friend, whom he murdered after he suggested he was a homosexual. And thus began a spate of alleged killings, for which Kelly would often linger in the aftermath.

Pointing out the majority of travellers would quickly leave the scene after such a distressing incident, Platt said: 'What got my attention was Mr Kelly often appeared to have been the only man left standing on the platform.'

He added Kelly would often volunteer false information to police – such as in one case that the victim had 'confessed' his wife had been having an affair before stepping in front of a train. As well as leaving the man's family confused and distraught, the surviving relatives would be unable to claim life insurance if the death was ruled suicide.

But Platt says police chiefs chose not to take action in a bid to avoid spreading panic among the public. He said: 'The Home Office decided this was not a case they wanted broadcasted.

'They felt that if it was broadcast, workers wouldn't go to work on the Northern Line, it was a Home Office policy decision: don't talk to the press and don't encourage the story.'

According to Platt, Kelly was investigated for 16 murders in total and acquitted of 8. He was also charged with attempted murder in 1982 for pushing an elderly man onto the tracks at Kensington Station but walked free due to a lack of evidence.

Having been charged with three murders unrelated to the Tube deaths (that of Boyd and two vagrants), it was also deemed to be not in the financial public interest to launch further proceedings against Kelly, Platt says.

He adds that a Freedom of Information request has revealed Kelly did not die in prison – though it is not known if he is still alive or died after his release.

A Scotland Yard spokesman told *The Huffington Post UK* the allegations were being dealt with by the British Transport Police (BTP).

A BTP spokesman said: 'We are aware of the claims included in this book but given the passage of time since they are alleged to have been committed these would prove difficult to substantiate without further evidence.

'We would invite Mr Platt to submit any information he has on these matters to us.'

Mail Online, December 2016

Homeless alcoholic double killer may be responsible for 31 deaths with unsuspecting victims SHOVED under Tube trains

Kieran Kelly was convicted of killing two men but could be linked to the deaths of some 29 others over more than three decades, a former police detective has claimed.

After moving from Dublin to London, Kelly, a homeless alcoholic, allegedly stalked victims on London Underground platforms before pushing them to their deaths.

Others were reportedly mutilated with broken wine bottles before being left to bleed to death.

The claims are the result of extensive research by Geoff Platt, a former acting detective constable who led the 1984 police investigation into Kelly.

Mr Platt has since published a number of books on the killer, including *London Underground Serial Killer: The Life of Kieran Kelly* which offers insight into Kelly's life and the chilling catalogue of his suspected crimes.

Since Mr Platt first published a book on Kelly in 2015 the family members of seven further potential victims have come forward to the British Transport Police, believing cases of suspected suicide might have been the work of Kelly.

Mr Platt claims Kelly targeted three different groups of people – gay men, police informants and men who reminded him of Mr Smith, his first victim – and used different methods to kill each.

Remains have also been recently unearthed at a property owned by Kelly in Dublin, Mr Platt said.

If he was responsible for the 31 deaths to which he has been linked, Kelly would have been one of Britain's most prolific serial killers.